CREATIVE POTTERY

PETER COSENTINO

CREATIVE POTTERY

PETER COSENTINO

TIGER BOOKS INTERNATIONAL
LONDON

This edition published in 1992 by
Tiger Books International plc,
London

ISBN 1 85501 267 7

copyright © 1985 Toppan Printing Co Ltd

Printed in Singapore

Contents

Foreword

This book is dedicated to my wife, Mandy, who gave so much time, as well as her unwavering support, and my children, Thomas and Matthew. A special mention must also go to my parents and sister for their continued encouragement. I would like to thank all the professional potters, and students, who have contributed their work to the book, and Victor Luton, whose love of pottery was passed on to me when I was his pupil. My thanks also to Christopher Gowing at Buckinghamshire County Museum for his help in selecting work from the museum. Finally, I would like to thank Philippa, Tony and Steve at the Paul Press, Andy, the photographer, and Darren Warner, his assistant for all their help.

My own introduction to clay some 20 years ago, when I was at school, was a memorable event and was to develop into an obsession for pottery of every kind. In **Creative Pottery** I have tried to provide a straightforward and practical guide to working with clay that will give you the same amount of pleasure, excitement and creative fulfilment I find in pottery.

I have often found that the early enthusiasm of many prospective potters is dampened when they first attempt to use clay, either because they are not taught properly, or because they are trying to make something which is simply too difficult for them. But after teaching students of different ages and abilities for 12 years, I have learned that the way to avoid, or at least overcome, these initial disappointments is to make every technique as clear and as simple as possible, and to ensure that every new working method comes as a natural progression from the one before. Every forming and decorative technique is explained in step-by-step sequences, and there are projects to help you consolidate what you have learnt. I have kept the use of technical terms to a minimum too, so as not to confuse you.

You should take what I say as guidance only, since every potter has his or her individual working methods. As you progress, you will find that you develop your own style. However, I have included, wherever possible, hints and tips that I have learnt over the years that you may find useful to adopt yourself – I have even suggested a few short cuts!

Mastering any craft requires practice and considerable patience, pottery being no exception. However, you will be amazed at how much you can achieve with relatively little experience. I have included examples of my students' work throughout the book to illustrate various aspects of pottery. Some of these were produced by students who had been learning pottery for less than 50 hours. The large coil pot with the dragon motif *(see p57)* was one student's first attempt at coiling, and was only the second piece of work he had ever made.

Finally, I do hope you will enjoy yourself as much as I have done with clay. You will find that you prefer some aspects of pottery to others, but don't let this stop you experimenting with other techniques. My own first love is the actual throwing process, but I still find the many other facets of pottery exciting.

Good luck and happy potting!

Understanding design

Design is an integral part of pottery – you cannot make a successful pot without an understanding of the process it involves. Beginners often feel that it is sufficient to master the basic techniques of forming, decorating and firing in the early stages, but this is not the case. It is inevitable that these aspects should have priority, but this should not mean that the all-important element of design should be neglected, since the two go hand in hand. You can make attractive and individual pieces of work with the minimum of technical competence, if you have planned your design well.

One of the most important facets of the design process is finding and interpreting sources and stimuli for design. Although it is impossible to provide an exhaustive list, I have suggested areas that are well worth exploring for design material, and how best to study them constructively, in this chapter. However, you should regard every suggestion as only a starting point for your own work. As you gain in confidence, try to explore your personal design ideas and develop an individual style.

It is a good idea to visit museums and galleries where there are good collections of historical and contemporary pottery. This will give you the chance to see how other potters have created successful designs by using shape, colour and texture, and how they approached and solved specific design problems. Concentrate on individual pieces of work, looking at what the potter has set out to achieve and assessing whether or not he has been successful.

I have tried to include in this chapter as wide a range as possible of different types of pottery to demonstrate the many possibilities open to you, the linking factor being that they are all successful designs. In each case I have indicated the sources, the techniques and the materials used to show how each element has been combined to form a complete and satisfying whole.

Understanding design

When you try to define what makes a successful piece of pottery – whether you are assessing your own work or someone else's – there are several considerations you ought to take into account, apart, of course, from your individual taste. The key question is what has the pot's creator set out to achieve? For instance, if he or she has made something functional, such as a cup and saucer, it can only be a success if it fulfils its function; if he or she has made a portrait bust, it will be a success if the likeness is accurate.

Abstract and non-functional work require different criteria, as they can only be judged on purely aesthetic terms. You should also take experience and technical competence into account – you should not judge the work of a beginner by the same standards as the work of an expert.

Regardless of the type or nature of any piece of pottery, your final evaluation must take into account whether the potential of the medium has been explored to the full – the most outstanding pieces of work will always stand out by being 'just right', a harmonious fusion of all the different elements of ceramics to form a perfect whole.

Mastering the basic forming and decorative techniques of pottery are inevitably the first priority for any beginner, but even when you make your first pot, these must go hand in hand with an appreciation of the considerations of design. Try to think about shape, size, proportion, colour and pattern and how you can best utilize both the potential of the clay itself and the enormous variety of ceramic techniques available to you. Every type of clay responds in a different way and every forming or decorative technique creates its own particular effect. You also have a vast range of colours and glazes at your disposal.

On the whole, people tend to think that artistic talent is a quality some people are born with and others are not. However, even for those who view themselves as unartistic and who are completely lacking in confidence, there are certain design principles and techniques that can be learned and that will enable you to produce attractive and individual pottery.

Burnished pot by Magdalene Odundo
The rich polished surface complements the simple and controlled shape, which is reminiscent of a gourd. The pot is earthenware; it was handbuilt and then the surface was burnished.

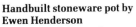

Handbuilt stoneware pot by Ewen Henderson
Forming and decoration need not always be separate elements in the ceramic process – here Ewen Henderson has combined both to great effect.

The pot is made from a composite body of different clays. These react together during firing to create exciting and unusual surface textures and colours. ◁

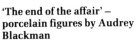

Set of jugs by Jane Hamlyn
Here, the shape of the traditional jug is given an adventurous and individual touch. The surface decoration and the fine quality of the pattern enhances Jane Hamlyn's lively use of form.◁

'The end of the affair' – porcelain figures by Audrey Blackman
Here Audrey Blackman has used the posture of the figures to suggest character and emotion – she does not feel the need to use faces. Her figures are perfectly balanced and are given extra stability by their layered structure.

The skeletons of these figures are made from rolled clay. Thin clay sheet is then wrapped around the skeleton to fill out the figure. ▷

Teapot, cups and saucers by Sabina Teuteberg
This stoneware set was decorated with bold abstract patterns inspired by musical rhythms, in particular those of jazz. The pattern is created by laying pieces of coloured clay on to the surface. ▷

The design process

Design inspiration can come from any source – a landscape, a leaf, machinery, the texture of a piece of wood or cloth, a newspaper, a photograph, a book or just the imagination. Any piece of source material is open to a variety of interpretations and it is up to you to explore the possibilities it offers.

Having chosen your source material, you should begin to develop your design ideas on paper, making rough sketches, taking notes about your source's particular qualities and character and trying to think how these can best be evoked in clay. (This is particularly important if the source material you are using is not always readily available.)

When you are satisfied with the design you have produced on paper, you must select appropriate clays, colourants, glazes and decide which techniques to use in order to make and decorate it to good effect. Draw up an outline of the working process it will involve, beginning to end, showing at which stages colour, texture and glazing should be added.

Although you should always explore any design idea thoroughly before beginning work, try to reassess your original concept continually as the actual piece of pottery or sculpture develops. Stand back from your work occasionally and look at it critically – is the design evolving as you first imagined? If not, where have you gone wrong?

Textured vase by Peter Cosentino
This piece of work evolved from studies made of a peach pip to explore its design potential. The basic shape was thrown and then beaten to produce a slightly flatter body before more clay was added to create the heavily-textured surface.

A matt white dolomite glaze was used. This was brushed with copper and manganese oxide to enhance the surface texture.

There will inevitably be times when you are not satisfied with your work, and when you have passed the stage of being able to alter it. Yet the occasional failure can be very constructive. Try to analyse where and why your idea has not worked, so that you do not make the same mistakes again.

Choosing your materials and techniques
You should always think carefully when choosing the clay, the decorative and firing techniques, the colours and the glazes you use for any piece of ceramic work. They are all vital to its success. But how do you know which are the right materials? To a large extent, trial and error are the only ways in which you can learn.

Rounded pots by Peter Cosentino
The design for these thrown pots was developed from observations of puffballs. To create the surface effect required, the pots were burnished and then biscuit fired, before being smoke fired. The smoke firing was carefully controlled to produce the variegated colouring, which is such an important decorative feature.

Throughout this book, I have tried to indicate, as far as possible, which type of clay is best suited to which forming method and what sort of effects different decorative techniques and glazes create. Use this information, and try to think of your work as a whole, with every different element perfectly integrated.

The search for inspiration
Potters whose work reflects a striking individual style or approach are frequently asked what inspires them. The answers are always different and often surprising. Inspiration comes from both the most ordinary and extraordinary sources.

It is worth keeping any source materials you find particularly stimulating in your studio, although you should avoid cluttering your work area. Keep a small and changing display in a place set apart specifically for the purpose.

There are two basic types of source material: primary source material, which is any source material experienced at first hand; and secondary source material, which is any material you experience at second hand. Such material includes television and radio programmes, films, plays, and books, newspapers, magazines and journals of every kind.

Slab pot by Val Barry
Slab construction lends itself to simplicity of shape. The pot comes from a series whose shapes were inspired by the sails of Chinese junks. △

Porcelain pot by Mary Rogers
Here Mary Rogers has carefully chosen her medium to reflect the translucency and delicacy of closed overlapping petals. The rim of the pot was left untrimmed to enhance the naturalness of its form. ▷

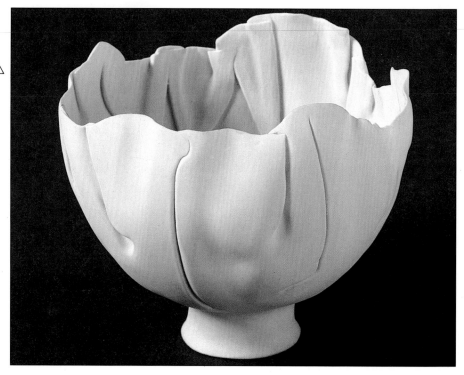

Images from nature

The natural world provides an inexhaustible supply of visual images; its shapes, textures, patterns and colours all translate beautifully into ceramic terms. Search along the seashore for seaweed, shells, pebbles, fossils, or even beached marine life, such as starfish and sea anemones. Make studies of the trees, flowers, vegetables, fruits and grasses you have in your garden or can find in the nearby countryside. You can also try drying some of these to see how their character changes through the process. Look out for interesting forms of fungi and cacti, which often produce extraordinary shapes and textures.

You can study your source material in minute detail, concentrating on the finer qualities of a stem, a petal or a pip. Alternatively, try using a whole tree or plant as an inspiration for a design.

Images from the mechanical and man-made world

Tools, machinery, musical instruments, children's toys, kitchen utensils and a variety of everyday objects found in any average home can prove to be useful and often unexpected sources of stimuli. Fabrics and materials of every kind, from silk to leather, can provide a basis for exploring pattern and for suggesting designs suitable for surface decoration, while clothes and footwear can also suggest new shapes and textures.

Ideas from the world around us

Our environment can often be a marvellous source of

'Predator form' by Ruth and Alan Barrett-Danes
The fantasy predator has evolved from observations of birds, humans and reptiles. The base of this stoneware piece is made from an enclosed thrown sphere, which is then softened to take the predator form. △

Stoneware pot by Mary Rogers
The surface design and glaze texture evoke the qualities and patterns widely found in nature from shells to seedpods. The pot was handbuilt. ◁

Press-moulded slab pot by James Tower
Patterns found in nature, such as the veining in rocks, and the eddying of the sea, inspired the decoration on this earthenware pot. The rich decorative effect has been produced by using sgraffito on the white glaze to reveal the dark glaze beneath.

inspiration, although all too often many of us are not fully aware of the visual potential on our own doorstep. Every environment offers something completely different, both visually and atmospherically. Contrast a rural landscape, with its natural lines and textures, its muted colours, and its sense of space, with an urban landscape, where roads and buildings dominate, where the colours are bold, and where the noise and bustle of people, cars and buses fill every scene. Study the lines of the architecture, the attitudes of bus queues, the shapes of vehicles. Buildings, in particular, offer great scope for developing slabbed forms.

Museums and galleries

Although there is no substitute for the first-hand experience of trying various techniques for yourself, anyone interested in pottery and ceramics should visit museums and galleries as much as possible to see how potters have worked throughout history. Exhibitions of contemporary ceramics may also be found in libraries as well as commercial galleries.

Many students visiting museums for the first time mistakenly assume that all their thoughts and efforts should be concentrated on ceramic collections. However, museums not only provide interesting collections of ceramics, but also offer other sources of visual stimuli – memorabilia, everyday objects and artefacts from different cultures and different eras.

If you are looking at the products of a specific historical period, try to assimilate the preoccupations and beliefs of that particular society and see how these affected its art. Study tools, weapons and jewellery as potential design sources. Natural history sections of museums, with their collections of skeletons, preserved life, fossils and rocks, can also prove interesting.

The main disadvantage of studying exhibits in museums or galleries is their remoteness, and the fact that they cannot be handled. This is a great pity, particularly with ceramics, as only by holding and touching them can you fully appreciate the subtler qualities of weight, shape and texture. Occasionally, by prior arrangement, special parties may be allowed to handle exhibits, but this depends upon the individual gallery or museum. Commercial galleries sometimes permit handling.

Making the most of a museum visit

Always allow yourself as much time as possible for your visit and always take a sketchbook and crayons or pencils. If you live close to the museum, you will find you gain more from short but regular visits.

Use your sketchbook to record as much information as possible from any source materials that may appeal to you. Make studies of any interesting detail and

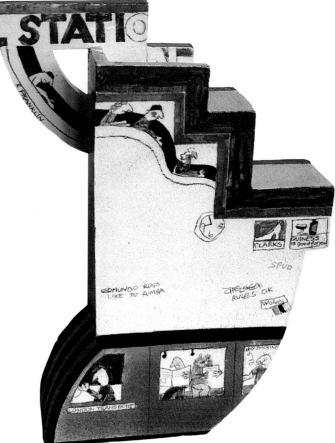

Underground pot by Ruth Franklin
The hustle and bustle of urban life is captured in this sculptural piece. The outline of the form provides a perfect framework for its pictorial content. This slab pot is earthenware and decorated with underglaze decoration and transparent glaze.

Porcelain bowl by Peter Lane
In direct contrast to Ruth
Franklin's work, this bowl
evokes the quiet qualities of a
rural environment. The
design of the vertical rows of
pierced holes was suggested
by a mountain waterfall.

particular shapes; explore the different methods of
construction that might be used to recreate them in
clay, and make a note of any specific decorative
techniques that could be used to achieve a certain
texture or pattern. Some museums will allow their
exhibits to be photographed but it is unlikely that you
will be allowed to use flash. In any case you should ask
permission before you take any photographs.

Secondary source material
Drawings, paintings, photographs, illustrations,
newspapers, books, magazines, television and film
represent the main sources of secondary source
material, providing an enormous amount of
information. News headlines, a fairy tale, or a poem
may trigger off an idea for a sculpture; a famous
painting may suggest a new interpretation of its subject;
and even maps, or the diagrams found in scientific
books, can give you unexpected inspiration.

The very nature of secondary source material means that, unlike primary source material, it is used as an indirect source of inspiration – it is rarely a question of simply copying a design, but rather one of how you interpret an idea in design terms. For example, many complex ideas and images will be evoked by any one news story – how you use these, which particular ones you give prominence, and which ones you discard completely will decide the character of your work.

Secondary source material is particularly useful for sculptural work, as it provides an inexhaustible fund of ideas around which to base your work. However, it can be also used as a basis for surface decoration.

It is very useful to keep a collection of cuttings and photographs in your studio for reference, catalogued by subject. The following types of material are just a few suggestions: natural history books and photographs; geology and geography books and maps; scientific books and journals; paintings, drawings and photographs of land, sea and townscapes; paintings, drawings and photographs of machines, cars, trains, planes; graphics and technical drawings; photographs, drawings and plans of buildings and architecture; famous paintings, drawings or sculptures; magazines and periodicals of every kind; newspapers; poetry; fairy tales; classic stories.

Recording information

Try to record as much information as possible from your source material before you begin work. This will make you look at it closely and critically and will often reveal interesting details, which you might otherwise miss. You will also find that it helps generally to

Toothpaste tube by Rebecca Peters (student)
This piece of work is realistic in every respect, except for its size, being about 90cm (36in) long. The basic form is made from wrapped slabs; these were then pressed to suggest the characteristic qualities of a squeezed toothpaste tube. A combination of coloured slips and colouring oxides were used under a transparent glaze. ▽

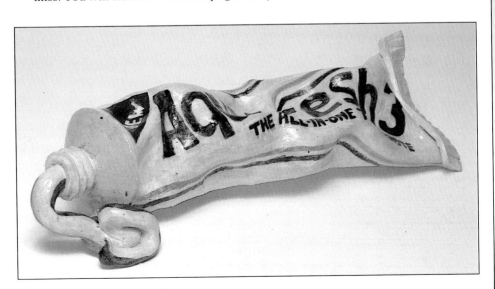

Nut and bolt by Delan Cookson
When taken out of context, even the most mundane objects can create a powerful impact. This piece of ceramic sculpture incorporates slab construction and thrown elements. Delan Cookson interferes with the surface as little as possible so that the natural qualities of the clay can reveal themselves. ◁

Laced pot by Delan Cookson
Fabric and textiles can be used as a source of inspiration, whether they are taken from costumes in museums or from your own wardrobe. This thrown pot uses a laced effect as its main decorative feature. ▽

21

△
Picnic with tiger by Hilary Brock
Hilary Brock draws his design ideas from, amongst other sources, Edwardian theatrical postcards, fairground organs and the silent cinema. He builds up a mental vocabulary by browsing through books and magazines or even watching historical plays on television.

increase your awareness of shape, form, texture and pattern. Information can be recorded by sketching, taking photographs, or – to a limited extent – by making notes. It is often useful to use a combination of all these.

Sketching
This is perhaps the best way of recording information, but it can only provide a two-dimensional impression of your source material. If you are using the source for a sculpture or clay form, rather than just surface decoration, you will have to sketch your source material from a variety of angles and viewpoints in order to recreate as full an image as possible.

When detail is not necessary, try to concentrate on capturing the shape and structure. If necessary, break the form down into a series of simple rough geometric shapes initially, then add further detail to the outline. When specific details, patterns or textures do need to be recorded accurately, concentrate on small areas. For example, cut open a red cabbage, and examine the complexities of the leaf folds. You will be able to see that a square inch of such a material can offer a whole series of patterns for surface decoration. Try to sketch this in the most minute detail possible.

You do not have to be an excellent artist to be able to record design information adequately or effectively. However, it is necessary to practise sketching, as it is a vital part of the design process.

Burnished dish by Siddig El'Nigoumi
Siddig El'Nigoumi was born in the Sudan and his work is heavily influenced by Arabic calligraphy and by everyday Islamic and African patterns and symbols. This press-moulded dish is earthenware and has been decorated with a sgraffito design. ◁

For your work materials, a spirally-bound A4-size sketchbook is the best all-round choice, and pencil is probably the most convenient medium. If you do use pencil, it is worth having a wide range of different types, but in any case you will need a pencil with a medium soft lead, such as a 2B.

Pencil or pen and ink are the best media to use for making detailed sketches. If you want to concentrate on general outlines or simplified and basic shapes, charcoal, pastels or chalk are more effective. As these smudge, you should always spray your work with a fixative when you have finished it. Water colours can also be used for sketching, if you prefer. Whichever media you use, practise with it on different subjects to find out both its strong points and its limitations.

Plate by Alan Frewin
Portraits are rarely found on plates, but in this unusual piece of work the shape of the plate provides the perfect frame for the picture. The plain blue and white colouring of the portrait gives this plate a classic simplicity. It was created by painting cobalt and manganese over white tin glaze before being once fired.

Nude study and pot by Eric Mellon
The watercolour study of the reclining nude is used as a basis for the colouring oxide decoration on the pot. Eric Mellon draws both from literary sources – especially mythology – and his studies of life.

Photography

Photography saves time and effort when recording source material, and is invaluable when it is neither convenient nor practical to use a sketchbook. Most cameras can produce reasonable landscape, environmental and general reference shots. For recording a wide range of different information with good quality and detail, a 35mm single lens reflex camera is the best all-round choice.

A camera can capture a moment, or a transient expression or movement that would be impossible to catch with a sketchbook. It also enables you to record accurate information about your source material from an almost unlimited number of viewpoints. This makes it particularly useful for studies of people or animals. Live models are also not always available for long enough periods of time for you to sketch them properly or work directly from them, unless you have the opportunity to attend life classes. In such cases, photographs are again ideal for reference.

It is worth building up a library of photographs – both your own and those of others – to use as source material. Even if you do not work directly from them, they often provide useful starting points for designs.

Drawing from life

Clay is an extremely versatile medium. It can be sculpted in the likeness of a person or animal and modelled to recreate the qualities of skin and fur. Clay surfaces can be textured to look like wood, metal, leather or fabric, thereby making lifelike representations of almost anything, from a pair of boots to a pencil sharpener, possible.

To be able to reproduce a faithful image of a person or object, you must make detailed studies of it, using sketches, photographs and notes. Where necessary, you should also make notes on proportions and measurements. Try experimenting with texture and colour on the clay surface to see how closely you can mimic the quality of the original.

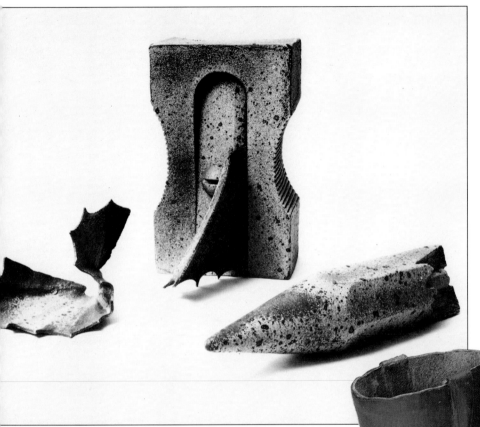

Pencil sharpener by Delan Cookson
Delan Cookson sees in clay a medium that is a natural mimic of all kinds of materials both hard or soft. In this piece of work, clay is used to imitate wood, graphite, metal and plastic. ◁

Boots by Graham Legge (student)
These stoneware boots again demonstrate the versatility of clay. They are constructed from slabs, painted in black slip and left unglazed to reproduce the quality of leather. The insides of the boots are lightly sprayed with manganese. ▽

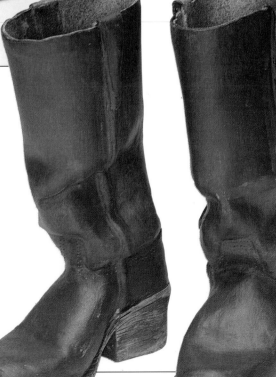

Experimenting with clay texture
Sketching is a technique rarely associated with clay. This is a pity, as it is quite easy and can be used both for experimenting with texture and for pictorial imagery.

Roll out a slab of clay about 1cm (⅖in) thick (see p60), and place it on a work board that is slightly larger than the slab itself, and which should be covered with newspaper or sacking so that the clay can easily be removed after you have finished.

Choose the object or scene you want to sketch, and approach your slab of clay as a painter would his or her canvas. Experiment with as many of your available tools (see pp50-1) as possible and draw, cut, carve, model, texture, or build on the clay surface until you feel you have created the impression you want.

If it is possible, it is well worth working outside the studio, sketching landscapes, buildings, flowers or wildlife. (Remember to take all the relevant tools with you and a chair to sit on.) Using such a direct approach to sketching often makes you study your subject more closely than you would otherwise, and will help you to capture the spirit and immediacy of the environment around you.

You can approach sketching outside as a painter would working on location, aiming to produce an almost complete piece of work, which only requires a few finishing touches when you return to the studio. The slab on which you have worked can then be decorated further, or simply fired, to make a decorative plaque. Alternatively, you can use sketching as another method of recording information, as it produces a more vivid and more accurate reference source than an ordinary two-dimensional sketch would.

Painting on clay

The clay surface can be seen simply as a canvas to be painted. Some potters use the techniques learnt as painters to decorate their work with pictorial images, but using oxides, slips or glazes instead of oils

Plate by Alan Frewin
The design inspiration for this painted plate came from the drawings of Gustav Klimt and shows the versatility and detail possible with painting on clay. The plate was first covered with white slip. When this was completely dry, slips coloured with underglaze colours and body stains were painted over it with a brush. Glaze was then sprayed over the picture. ▽

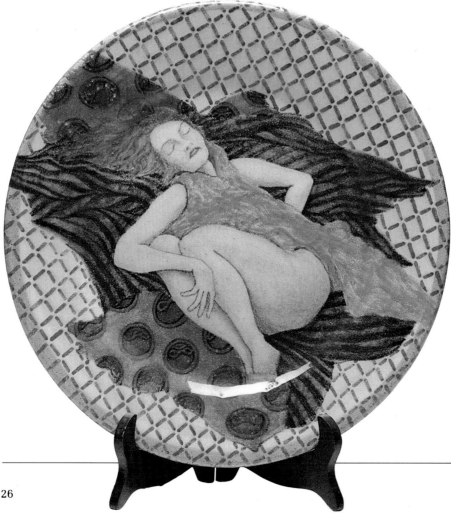

Tile mural by Maggie Berkowitz
Sunflowers and exotic settings are recurrent themes in this potter's work. Her designs are loosely worked out on paper and then translated into vivid images on a canvas of blank industrially-produced tiles. The picture is created by brushing and trailing layer after layer of glazes and oxides on to the tiled surface, which often necessitates several firings. ◁

or watercolours. Brushed pictorial designs of this kind are especially suited to tiled plaques or walls, or slabs, as a flat surface is ideal for the type of decoration produced by these techniques. However, they need not be limited to this area of ceramics. A picture can be set inside a bowl or dish, for example, to great effect, when the curving edges of the form are used to complement the shapes and lines of the painted design.

Choosing shapes and forms

When you are looking for source materials for new designs for ceramic forms, such as vases, jugs, or bowls, try to find objects whose shapes are evocative – a gently swelling gourd can suggest the shape for the body of a tea pot; a seed pod may suggest the perfect neck for an unusual bottle; an opening bud may translate beautifully into the rim of a vase.

Once you have found a source idea that appeals to you, before you begin work you must make sure it fulfils all the necessary practical considerations in addition to looking attractive. Stability, balance and proportion are fundamental to any piece of pottery. Also, when you find a particular shape or form that is successful in both these respects, use it as a theme to be developed with variations.

Use the surface decoration as an extension and complement of your work's shape. For example, if the shape of your work is inspired by a flower, you could incise the surface to evoke the qualities of overlapping or folding petals. If your work is inspired by a landscape, you can use textures, colours and glazes which suggest the natural world.

Sketched designs and pots by David Morris
The lively sketches illustrate how the potter experiments with subtle differences in form and decoration. This type of exploratory design work lies behind the pots shown (right). Note how the fluid decorative brushwork complements the gentle curved shape of the pots.

Designing functional pottery

The design of any functional piece of pottery is limited quite stringently by the fact that it must, first and foremost, be able to perform the function for which it is intended – for example, you must be able to hold and pour a tea pot easily for the design to be considered successful. The more specific the function of a pot, the more constraints on the design there will be.

An enormous amount of trial and error is necessary to create a new but functional design, and usually beneath any innovation in this particular area the traditional outlines can still be detected. When you experiment with designs for functional pottery, begin by making subtle alterations to the basic shapes and let new ideas evolve gradually. Use small but significant details – the position and shape of a handle or the type of lid, for example – to alter the character of your designs. They need not all be radically different.

Pot by Richard Batterham
This piece of work is a perfect example of classic simplicity and functional ware. Incised decoration is used to increase the impression of height. The subtle colouring and the quality of the glaze complement the shape to create a harmonious whole. △

Surrealism

You can use the same techniques you used to make realistic sculptures to create surrealistic sculpture. Objects or people can be reproduced in accurate and realistic detail, but the context in which they are used creates a completely different and unreal but vivid image. An ordinary, and usually insignificant object, such as a tube of toothpaste, can be enlarged to gigantic proportions; incongruous shapes and objects can be grouped together, and their relationships distorted; a sculpture, which at first seems entirely straightforward, can reveal, on second glance, an unexpected and entirely different angle.

Abstract design

Try experimenting with completely abstract forms and look out for interesting shapes, objects and ideas to use as source material. Use them as starting points for exploring new shapes and forms. Remove particular aspects of the source material that appeal to you from their context, so that they lose their original identity. Try developing a design from a source material that still conveys its individual qualities and character without

Stoneware form by Sheila Fournier
This layered abstract form shows both the influence of the traditional bowl and the qualities of an opening flower. The dark colouring complements the stark simplicity of shape. The form was handbuilt from heavily-grogged clay. △

Jelly press by Delan Cookson
This ingenious and witty sculpture turns the laws of reality upside down, as the iron strength of the press is defeated by a mere jelly. Slabbed clay was used for the press itself and blown glass for the jelly. ▷

'Parting lovers' by Rebecca Peters (student)
The traditional romantic theme of parting lovers is given a macabre twist in this clay sculpture. What at first appears to be a sentimental piece of work emerges, at a second glance, as a comment on the destructiveness of war.

31

Bowl by Gordon Baldwin
Here Gordon Baldwin has reassessed the traditional shape and idea of a bowl to create a purely non-functional form. The abstract design helps to highlight the break from tradition. ▷

there being any immediate likeness. For example, try to make a form that suggests the idea of machinery in motion, concentrating, say, on the ideas of movement and interaction. Always test any ideas on paper first, making sketches of how you envisage the design. Then translate the design into three-dimensional terms using simple clay maquettes to give you a rough idea of what the finished piece of work will look like.

Once you have explored the various forming and decorative methods, as well as the different aspects of ceramic design, it is only natural that some will appeal to you more than others. It is likely that you will eventually find that you prefer to concentrate on certain areas of pottery. It is important to develop an individual style but you should try not to restrict yourself too much – if you experiment with different forms and types of decoration, your designs as well as your technical ability will improve. You will find that the more experienced you become, the more you will be able to use the versatility of clay to create effectively-designed pieces of work. New ideas for work also evolve naturally as you work. Every pot or sculpture you make will suggest either a new possibility in the same direction, or a completely new idea.

Composite pot by Hans Coper
This perfectly-balanced piece of work combines two separately-thrown elements in harmony. The subtle surface textures are created with oxides and slips. ◁

Black pots by Peter Cosentino
This group of pots was a personal exploration of shape and texture, simple forms being combined with heavily-organized surface textures – the pots were not intended to be functional.

Black and white slips were used to create a dry surface texture, which was intended to complement the pots' sculptural qualities.

Design techniques/1

Once you have developed your own design on paper or found a design you would like to copy, you must translate it into ceramic terms. It is not always easy to turn an apparently effective design sketch into a piece of pottery but there are some simple design techniques you can use.

A design for surface decoration can be adjusted to suit the size and shape of any piece of work by the simple process of gridding; it can then be traced and transferred on to the clay surface. Clay forms can also be made precisely by using templates.

The sequences shown here will help you to explore the potential of your chosen design source and to develop an idea from the source material. These sequences are by no means inflexible, but do provide useful guides from which to work.

Tracing and transferring
A design can be traced on to tracing paper and then transferred on to the appropriate clay surface with little difficulty. Use a design with plenty of bold lines – try to avoid fussy or extremely delicate details.

Place the tracing paper over the design and draw round the outlines with a pencil. Prepare the clay surface, coating it with slip if you wish (see pp138-9), and allow it to dry until it has become leatherhard.

Lay the tracing over the clay surface, with the pencil outline facing upwards. Draw over the outline again with the pencil, pressing quite firmly so that you impress the outline faintly in the clay surface. When you have transferred the complete outline of the design on to the clay, remove the tracing paper. Draw round the lines with a pointed tool to make them more pronounced, or scratch out different areas within the design.

Transferring a design
1 Place the tracing in position, cutting it, if necessary, so it lies flat.

2 Pressing gently but firmly, trace around the outlines of the design with a pointed tool.

3 When you have finished, peel away the paper. The lines of the design should be marked lightly in the clay.

4 If you have coated the clay with slip, you can scrape away certain areas to show the clay beneath.

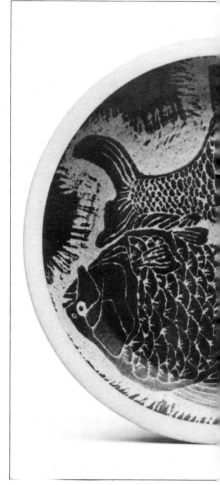

The finished design
Tracing and transferring a design provides the bare outline for decoration. You must also think carefully about which colours, textures and glazes to use. ▽

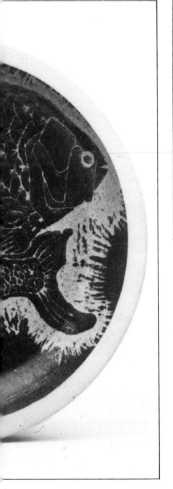

Gridding

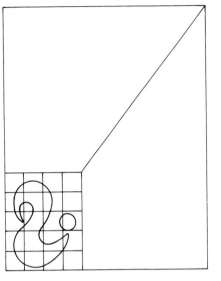
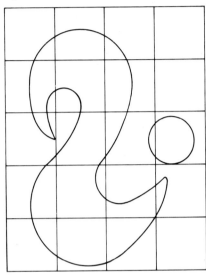

The size and shape of any design can be enlarged or altered by using the gridding method. Cover the design with a piece of tracing paper, and trace round the outlines of the design with a pencil. Divide the tracing paper into squares of either 1.2cm (½in) or 2.5cm (1in) – the smaller the square, the greater the accuracy of the finished product. Number each square for reference.

Divide another sheet of tracing paper into squares two, three times, or four times the original size, as you require. Then copy all of the outlines of the design square by square from the original grid on to the new one.

If you wish to make a design longer and narrower, redraw your grid into rectangles which are twice as long as the original squares, but of the same width. Transfer the outline of the original design to the new grid, square by square, as you did before.

Making templates
For tiles, plaques (see p61), or slab constructions (see pp66-7), it is advisable to make a template before cutting the shape you need. For tiles, plaques, or slab constructions, trace and transfer your chosen outline on to stiff card. Then cut cleanly round the outline with a scalpel. Place this template on the clay slab and draw lightly round it with a pointed tool. Remove the template and cut the shape out with a pottery knife. ▷

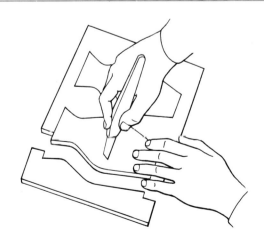

Design techniques/2

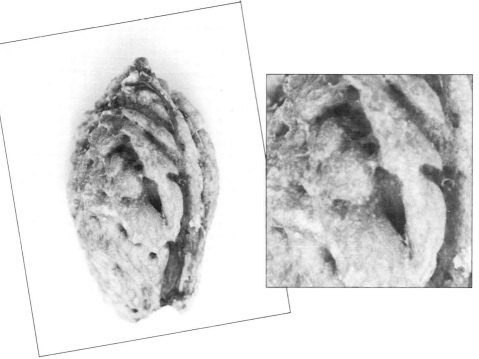

Developing designs

The sketches or photographs you take of your source material need not be used to produce representational designs. They can equally be used to produce patterns and designs of an abstract nature, which can be used to create attractive surface decoration. Drawings or photographs that contain plenty of detail are most likely to be successful when used as sources for abstract patterns.

Begin by isolating a small portion of a drawing or photograph. Enlarge it until you can see every detail quite clearly. Here, a photograph of a peach stone has been enlarged to reveal a textural quality that suggests many possibilities for exciting surface decoration.

Exploring design sources

New designs can be created by taking the main features from a piece of primary or secondary source material and developing it in different directions. For example, the stylized leaf (below) has a strong outline and is patterned with veins and spots. Each of these characteristics, or combinations of them, can be used as a starting point for developing a design.

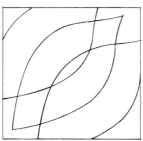

1 Isolate the basic outline of the leaf.

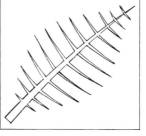

2 Concentrate on the veining of the leaf.

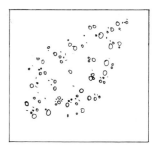

3 Study the smaller details of pattern and texture.

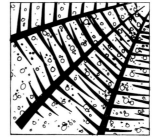

4 Develop a design from the leaf's surface patterns.

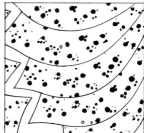

5 Combine surface patterns and outlines in a design.

Below are some suggestions for designing and making ceramic sculptures and pots. Each idea has deliberately been left open to individual interpretation and is only intended to provide a starting point.

None of the projects necessarily demands great expertise in pottery, and are suitable for any beginner. You can adapt each of them to be as simple, or as elaborate, as you wish.

Design Projects

Make detailed studies of a sleeping animal and develop a design for a coiled sculpture.

Create a set of related designs for candleholders, which are to be made from joined thrown sections. Explore a number of variations on your designs, and then choose the five or six most satisfactory ones for your actual work.

Explore a design for a set of six goblets for drinking wine or cider. Concentrate on creating a simple but functional form – the goblets should be comfortable to hold, easy and pleasant to drink from, and stable. Study some classic examples of goblets before you begin work.

Design a money box, which can be made from a basic pinched sphere (see pp54-5) in the form of an animal or bird. Concentrate on evoking the particular qualities and characteristics of your chosen animal using surface textures. Use photographs or drawings of the animal as source material.

Experiment with texture and colour on a clay slab before you begin work, until you are satisfied that you have captured the quality of the animal's hide or fur. When you make the money box itself, cut a slot in the top large enough to allow coins to be removed without breaking the box.

Enlarge sections from a range of different fabrics, so that you have a detailed image of its weave and the texture of the strands. Use these to develop a series of patterns that can be used for surface decoration.

Select a contrasting range of both natural and man-made objects or images. Make detailed studies of each, isolating what seem to you to be the most interesting characteristics. Create a design for a free-standing sculpture from these sources that shows either the man-made world in conflict with the natural world, or the two worlds combined in harmony.

Using the distinctive patterns found either in fossils or rock formations, develop a design for the surface decoration of a large thrown bowl or jar.

Working from ideas taken from news stories or current affairs – headlines, documentary films or magazine features all provide possible sources – develop a sculptural form that you feel reflects the modern world. You should try working from both visual and verbal sources, using abstract ideas as well as concrete images.

Study diagrams and magnified photographs of normally invisible organisms – examples of these can be found in any biological or medical reference book. Use these as a basis for evolving a design for a sculpture of a fantastical creature.

Explore the shape patterns apparent in a pile or scattering of matches or clothes pegs. Study the shapes of the spaces between each match or peg and ignore the details of the matches or pegs themselves. As you work, you will see that a random pattern begins to emerge – use this as a design for surface decoration of any thrown or slabbed form.

Make a life-size sculptural replica of any everyday domestic object of your choice. You should aim to create the illusion that your clay replica is real, concentrating on accurately reproducing the shape, texture and colour. Make detailed sketches of your model from a variety of angles, checking at every stage that the proportions are correct. Experiment as much as you can with textures and colours on a clay slab first until you feel you have captured the quality of the original as realistically as possible.

Use a vegetable as a source for the design of a casserole. You can create a surrealistic design, reproducing every detail of the vegetable faithfully but enlarging it in size. Alternatively, you can draw from your source material less specifically, using the patterns, shapes and textures as a basis for a design which simply evokes the qualities of the vegetable.

Design a plaque which is to be hung either in your kitchen or bathroom. Take the theme of 'underwater discovery' for the bathroom plaque or 'harvest festival' for the kitchen.

The medium and the method

I believe that if you left people to their own devices, they would discover most of the standard pottery techniques by themselves, simply by trial and error. Working in this way would also give them the chance to develop their own creative ideas and techniques without any preconceptions, or the constraints often imposed by formal teaching.

The great disadvantage of learning only by experience is that it takes time. I have tried here to eliminate the time-consuming element of trial and error while still encouraging people to experiment with their own ideas and working methods.

You will probably find that you master some techniques more quickly than others. However, you should try each technique – I have found that people often produce their best work using techniques they have initially disregarded completely. You should also remember that every working method is unique and that you cannot substitute one with another, as this will only result in second-rate work. Try instead to explore the individual qualities of every technique to the full.

You should start by learning as much as possible about how clay itself is formed, and how clay bodies are composed and manufactured, as this will help you to understand how and why clay behaves as it does. However, you do not have to learn any complicated technical data when you begin to study pottery – the practical aspects are far more important at this stage.

I have tried to use as simple and direct an approach in this section as possible, so that it can be easily understood by every beginner. For those who already have some knowledge or experience, or who are studying the subject at college or school, there are new and creative ideas based on familiar pottery techniques.

Working with clay/1

Clay possesses two vital properties that give it both an artistic and a practical appeal. First, it is plastic and easily workable, which means that it can be moulded to almost any shape or form you wish. Second, when clay is fired in extremely hot temperatures it becomes permanently hardened. This means that clay is an invaluable material for making functional pottery, such as jugs, cups and saucers, plates and bowls and also for creating works of art that will last for centuries.

The origins of clay
Clay comes from igneous rock, which forms when molten lava or magma hardens beneath or above the earth's surface. It is created by a long process of decomposition over hundreds of millions of years, as the rock is worn away by wind, water and snow above the ground, or corroded by water and acid below it.

Geologists divide clay into two basic types. The first is known as primary clay; this is clay that never leaves its site of origin. Primary clay contains few impurities, but is also relatively unplastic in its natural state, which makes it unsuitable for pottery. However, primary clay can be combined with other types of clay to make it more plastic and workable.

The second type of clay is known as secondary clay. This is clay that has been moved from its site of origin by rivers, glaciers, rain or wind. Secondary clay is usually plastic – that is, workable – and therefore suitable for pottery. It may also contain any number of different impurities, which may affect it in various ways. For example, if iron oxide is present in a clay, the clay will be red or red-brown in colour. The iron oxide will also affect the clay's firing temperature – clays with a large iron content cannot withstand high firing temperatures (see pp146-7).

The potter's medium
Clay in its natural state, whether primary or secondary clay, is not always suitable for pottery. Some types of clay are not plastic enough, while others may be too plastic. The colour of a particular clay may be unappealing, or it may require too high or too low a firing temperature. However, the natural properties of any clay can be altered or controlled by adding other substances. Clay manufacturers, or individual potters, mix clays with various other ingredients to make clay bodies to suit specific purposes. Porcelain and bone china are both familiar examples of artificially-produced clay bodies.

Although experienced potters often mix clay bodies to suit their own requirements, it is easier for beginners – at least initially – to buy a general all-purpose clay from a manufacturer, which is already prepared for use.

However, you may find that sometimes the clay you are using is too plastic, or shrinks and warps during drying or firing. These problems can be controlled by adding a substance called grog. This is clay that has been fired at a high temperature and then ground down to a fine powder. It can also be used to give strength and texture to the clay.

Grog is available in varying degrees of coarseness. The type you use depends on the size of the work you are undertaking – the larger the work, the coarser the grog should be. The coarseness of grog is measured in terms of the minimum size of mesh through which it will pass. For example, the smallest mesh through which a '40's' grog will pass will have 40 wires per linear inch.

The pottery process
Clay's physical state depends on the amount of water it contains. To work effectively, and to make good pottery, the potter has to be able to judge, and to be able to control, the amount of water in the clay.

Clay can only be worked, shaped and moulded when it is in its plastic state – at this stage it contains about 40 per cent water. Most of the pottery-forming processes – throwing, sculpting, pinching and coiling – can only be done while the clay is plastic.

The clay dries to become 'leatherhard' – that is, it is still impressionable, but barely pliable. At this stage, trimming and some decoration can take place, but the clay can no longer be shaped or moulded effectively. Eventually, as the clay dries further, it becomes what is known as 'greenware' – hard, brittle and fragile, and no longer impressionable. However, although greenware pottery may appear to be perfectly dry it still contains 20 per cent water. Although it may seem to be hard, it will soften and break down if it is placed in water.

To fix and harden any pottery permanently, it has to be fired in a kiln to remove the remaining water. This is the purpose of the biscuit firing, or the first firing, when the clay is fired in the kiln to a temperature between 950°C and 1000°C.

Choosing clay
Most amateur potters find it easier to work with a plastic, general-purpose manufactured clay than to prepare their own. Commercial clay should be reliable and should perform according to the manufacturer's description. However, do not restrict yourself to one type of clay; experiment with samples of other clays that appeal to you to give yourself a wider range of experience. Many suppliers offer sample packs of clay in very small quantities, and although this may be an expensive way of buying clay, it is useful for performing your own experiments. The manufacturer's

catalogue should state clearly the purposes for which a clay is intended, and the required firing temperature.

Buying from manufacturers' catalogues
Clay manufacturers' catalogues are full of useful information, and should be kept for reference. They are usually free, often lavishly illustrated with examples of contemporary ceramics and, more importantly, they give extensive descriptions of various clays and materials, and outline their particular qualities and uses. However, you should resist the temptation to buy any pottery tools or equipment before finding out whether you can make them yourself, buy them more cheaply from a non-specialist retail outlet, or even do without them.

Preparing clay
Plastic clay bought from a manufacturer has already been processed and should be ready for use. When clay

is quarried, it is usually crushed and then mixed with water to form a substance known as slip. It is then sieved and, if necessary, passed across electro-magnets to remove any iron particles. The slip is filtered, and then compressed to force out the water, leaving a plastic clay. This is either dried and crushed to a powdered form, or processed in a pugmill to make sure it is thoroughly mixed.

Even if you buy your clay from a manufacturer, you must check that it is in good working condition. The consistency of clay depends on its water content, and it is vital that the water is distributed evenly throughout the clay before you begin work. You should also make sure that there are no air pockets – trapped air can cause the clay to crack, or even explode, during firing.

To check that the clay is in good condition, cut off a section and slap it down – do not let it land with the freshly-cut side down – on a porous surface. Any faults – cracks, fractures or soggy patches – should now be

Reclaiming clay

1 Break up any dry clay into pieces as small as possible – this will help it to slake down more quickly. Pour water over the broken pieces of clay. ▷

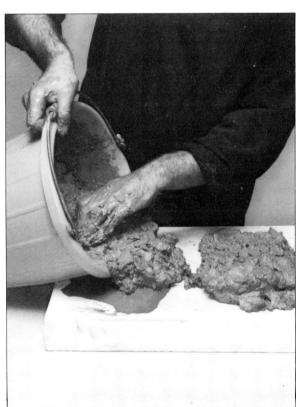

2 When the clay has completely broken down into slurry, drain, scoop or sponge away the excess water. Sieve the slurry if you are preparing locally-dug clay.

3 Spread the clay on a plaster slab or wooden board, and leave it to dry. When the clay is sufficiently dry, turn it over regularly to help it dry more quickly.

Working with clay/2

clearly visible. If there are faults, you must knead and wedge the clay before use.

Reclaiming clay
If you have bought powdered clay, have dug your own, or are reclaiming waste or dried clay, you should prepare it in the following way. However, clay cannot be reprocessed once it has been biscuit fired.

Find a suitably large watertight container. Break up any dry clay into the smallest pieces possible, and put them inside the container. Cover the clay with water, leaving it until the clay breaks or 'slakes' down into a slurry, and settles to the bottom of the container, leaving the excess water on top. This process usually takes about a day or so. Then drain, scoop, or sponge off as much of the water as possible. If you are preparing clay that you have dug yourself, which usually contains many impurities, you should sieve it. To do this, mix the clay slurry into a stiff paste and pass the mixture first through a coarse-meshed sieve. Then pass it through a fine sieve of about 80 mesh, to remove all the coarse grit and small stones.

Spread the clay slurry out on to a plaster slab, or a wooden board, if a plaster slab is not available. Leave the slurry to dry out, remembering to turn the whole clay mass periodically, once the underside has dried enough to be safely lifted. If you are using a plaster slab, the clay should be turned by hand – never use tools on it, as inevitably some plaster will break off and impregnate the clay. Turn the clay regularly to allow it to dry evenly. Once the clay is dry enough to be lifted cleanly from the slab without too much of it sticking to your hands, it is ready to be prepared for use. This is done by kneading and wedging.

If you have a pugmill, this can be used to mix and compress the clay. When the clay is dry enough to handle, prepare it by kneading and wedging it as described below. This should be done on a slate or concrete slab, positioned at waist height.

Kneading
You knead clay in almost exactly the same way as you would dough, but the principle is to work any air out of the clay, instead of into it. Initially, practise by

Kneading
Roll the clay into the shape of a swiss roll and turn the roll to face you lengthways on. Take hold of the end furthest from you, and pull it back towards you, folding the clay over. Press firmly down and away from your body, forcing the bent roll of clay in on itself. Use your palms, not your fingertips, as the latter will probably create small pockets of air. Repeat the whole process several times until you find that the clay has grown too long to handle comfortably. Then turn the clay so that you are facing it lengthways on again. Continue kneading it until the clay is of an even consistency throughout. This basic kneading technique is known as the 'ox' or 'bull head' method, because the imprints your hands leave form the clay mass into a shape that vaguely resembles a bull's head. ▷

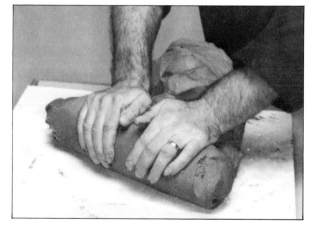

Wedging
This helps to ensure that the clay is free of air pockets. As with kneading, you should work initially with small quantities of clay, until you feel capable of coping with larger amounts – wedging can be very strenuous work. Wedge the clay on a concrete slab, not on a plaster one, as the process involves slamming the clay down and the force needed could easily split the plaster.

If the clay continually sticks to the wedging surface, it is too wet and soft and should be left to dry further before you resume wedging. You should also avoid wedging clay on the same point of the slab or board all the time, as the area quickly becomes saturated with water from the clay. This in turn will make the clay stick.

It is not possible to over-wedge clay, although prolonged wedging on a porous surface may eventually make the clay too dry for use. Although this is unlikely, if it does occur, you will have to mix the clay with a little water until it is plastic enough again to work.

kneading about 5kg (11lb) of clay, and then increase the amount until you feel you cannot physically cope with any more – kneading clay can be very tiring. Additives, such as grog and sand, colouring oxides and stains (see pp136-7), should be added during kneading.

Slice the clay into layers, sprinkle the additive between each layer, and knead together as before. If the clay sticks to the board or slab when you begin kneading, allow it to dry a little more. Alternatively, you can knead the clay on a plaster slab, which will absorb any excess moisture as you work.

Kneading can also be used to soften clay that is too stiff to work by slicing the stiff clay into rough layers, adding soft clay between each layer. Knead the whole mass as before and repeat the process until it becomes completely soft.

Storing clay

Once the clay has been prepared – whether you prepare it yourself or buy it – it should be stored carefully to ensure that it stays in prime condition. The most important point to remember is to stop the water in the clay evaporating.

Clay suppliers pack their clay in tough polythene sacks. This will prevent any water evaporating and, provided that the sacks do not become torn or split, the clay can be left in them and stacked outside in a damp and sheltered position. However, if you intend to leave the clay outside for a long time, you should cover it with a tarpaulin, or keep it in storage units. The latter can be bought from clay suppliers.

The ideal place to store clay in sacks is in a cool damp cellar, or outbuilding. However, if the clay is left for any length of time, it will need further preparation (that is, kneading and wedging) before it can be used.

If you leave clay in a warm room for an hour, or sometimes even less, it will dry out noticeably, so always take the simple precaution of wrapping any prepared clay you are not using in thin polythene. Take it out only when you are going to use it immediately. Small amounts of prepared clay can be kept in the studio in plastic bins, covered in polythene and a tight-fitting lid. It is important that the bins are airtight, as clay will dry out inside quite quickly.

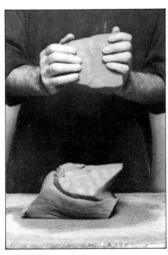

1 Take a piece of clay and, holding it comfortably in both hands, raise it to head height, and then slam it down forcefully on to the wedging surface. Lift the clay off the slab, turn it through 90° and slam it down on the surface again. Turn the clay through a further 90°, slam the clay down, rotate it again, and slam the clay down once more. △

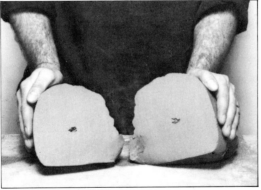

2 You should now have a four-sided block, each side of the clay mass having hit the surface in turn. Continue wedging, until the clay has become too thin to handle. Slice the clay into two or three sections with a cutting wire and slap the pieces together hard, to prevent air being trapped between them. Repeat the wedging process. Cut through the block with wire and check the inside surfaces for any air pockets. ◁

3 If the clay is being recycled, you should also look out for any pieces of debris as these must be removed before you can continue wedging. If any air pockets are present, continue wedging the clay until they have all been completely eliminated. ◁

Setting up a home studio/1

Few people are ever in a position to be able to set up a purpose-built pottery studio of their own. Initially, most amateurs have to make do with improvising tools and equipment until they can afford specific items, and with converting their garage, outhouse or garden shed into a workplace. This may not be ideal, but you can usually create a perfectly functional studio from what you already have available.

The studio

A self-contained studio is vital. It is neither practical nor hygienic to produce anything more than the occasional small pot in your house. Furthermore, you will need somewhere to keep unfinished work out of harm's way. Ideally, your studio should be at ground level, for convenience and for safety if the kiln is installed there; it should allow easy access for equipment and materials – wide or double doors are particularly useful.

Space and light

Space and light are the most important factors to be taken into consideration when planning a studio. You need as much space as possible: a floor area of 240 x 240cm (96 x 96in) is a realistic minimum. However, if your studio is this small, the kiln should be sited elsewhere, as the heat it creates will dry out prepared plastic clay, and may spoil your work in progress. The studio should be as well lit as possible, ideally with large windows. It is always preferable and more pleasant to work in natural light than under artificial lighting. If you do have to rely on artificial lighting, use the brightest possible.

Water and electricity

It is not essential to have running water actually in the studio, as long as a supply is reasonably close to hand. If you do have a studio with a water supply and sink, or if you intend to install one, the waste pipe should be led through a clay trap to prevent any clay from blocking the drains. If running water is unavailable, keep a supply to hand in a large plastic container.

An electricity supply is vital both for lighting and for other equipment. Plan well in advance where your kiln and wheel are to be positioned (if they are electrically operated), and have electric points installed within easy reach.

Frost damage

Freezing winter temperatures can be a potter's worst enemy, if a studio is not kept sufficiently warm. Freshly-thrown clay contains so much water that, when the water freezes, it expands and fractures the clay. Then, when the pot eventually thaws, it inevitably

Pinboard
Keep a pinboard for displaying reference and source material.

Damp cupboard
This should be airtight and non-porous and is used for storing work in progress to keep it damp. A plastic-coated metal filing cabinet makes an ideal damp cupboard.

Ventilator
An air ventilator ensures that the studio is well aired.

Window
The studio should be as well lit as possible – natural light is always best.

Concrete slab
This is a perfect surface for wedging clay.

Sink
An easily-accessible water supply is essential.

Cleaning equipment
You will need sponges, brushes, dustpans, mops and rubbish bins for the studio. You should not use these elsewhere in the house.

Shelves
Keep work in progress away from the kiln in the coolest part of the studio.

Clay bins
You need three large bins for storing and preparing clay – one to collect dry clay, one to slake down clay, and one in which to store prepared clay.

Bucket
This catches water draining from the wheel.

Wheel
An electric wheel is a good choice for beginners.

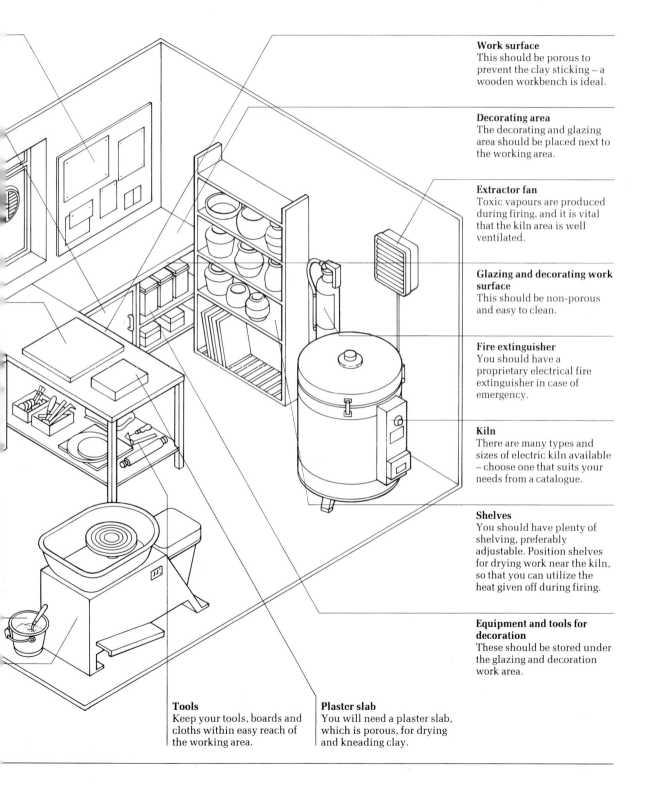

Work surface
This should be porous to prevent the clay sticking – a wooden workbench is ideal.

Decorating area
The decorating and glazing area should be placed next to the working area.

Extractor fan
Toxic vapours are produced during firing, and it is vital that the kiln area is well ventilated.

Glazing and decorating work surface
This should be non-porous and easy to clean.

Fire extinguisher
You should have a proprietary electrical fire extinguisher in case of emergency.

Kiln
There are many types and sizes of electric kiln available – choose one that suits your needs from a catalogue.

Shelves
You should have plenty of shelving, preferably adjustable. Position shelves for drying work near the kiln, so that you can utilize the heat given off during firing.

Equipment and tools for decoration
These should be stored under the glazing and decoration work area.

Tools
Keep your tools, boards and cloths within easy reach of the working area.

Plaster slab
You will need a plaster slab, which is porous, for drying and kneading clay.

Setting up a home studio/2

collapses. To prevent such disasters, you should install a small, thermostatically-controlled heater in your studio which should switch on when the temperature falls to near freezing.

Studio organization
Unless your studio has been purpose-built, you may not be able to design it precisely the way you want. However, you should try to plan it so that it allows you to progress naturally and logically through the working sequence of making pottery.

You will need three large plastic bins for storing clay – one for collecting dry clay that can be re-used; one for slaking down clay *(see pp40-1)*; and one with a tight-fitting lid for storing prepared clay that is ready for use. A plaster slab is needed for drying clay and a concrete slab for wedging *(see pp42-3)*. A sturdy work

bench for clay preparation and working, with a porous surface, is essential; it is also advisable to have shelves and a damp cupboard for storing work in progress. The wheel should be placed near or inside the preparation or working area. Working tools and cleaning equipment should also be stored here.

Plaster is a useful material for most potters and is used both to make work slabs and for making moulds *(see pp70-1)*. However, if it contaminates the clay, it spoils it, so if you anticipate using plaster in large quantities, you should set aside a space well away from the clay preparation and working areas.

The area for decorating and glazing should be separate from the preparation and working area. You will need a non-porous surface that is easy to clean on which to work. Necessary materials and tools should be stored close at hand; powdered raw materials used for

Electric kilns
These are available in a variety of sizes and may be either front loading or top loading. (The kilns shown are manufactured by Potclay Kilns Ltd.)

staining, colouring or glazing must be kept in a dry place, ideally in airtight jars.

You will need more shelving – preferably adjustable – for drying your work, and for storing biscuit fired pots or glazed ware waiting to be fired. Drying shelves should be positioned near the kiln to make use of the heat given off during firing. However, do not place the shelves too close to the kiln, as too much heat may dry the clay too quickly, causing it to warp, or damage or burn the shelves. The kiln should be sited well away from your store of damp plastic clay that is ready to use, the preparation area and the damp cupboard where unfinished work is stored.

Resources area
Whatever the size of your studio, you should try to allow some space for reference and source material as inspiration for your own creativity. Here you should keep relevant books and publications, *objets trouvés*, working sketches, future designs and any other ideas you may find useful. A couple of shelves and a pinboard should be sufficient for your needs. If possible, keep one or two pieces of your own finished work in the resources area, so that you can constantly assess your own progress.

Equipment
There are various pieces of pottery equipment and machinery available. However, many of them are not necessary for the amateur potter, so you should always think carefully before making any major investment. Blungers (machines that liquidize clay into slip), pugmills, which can prepare large amounts of clay for use in a short time, and rollers for rolling clay slabs are

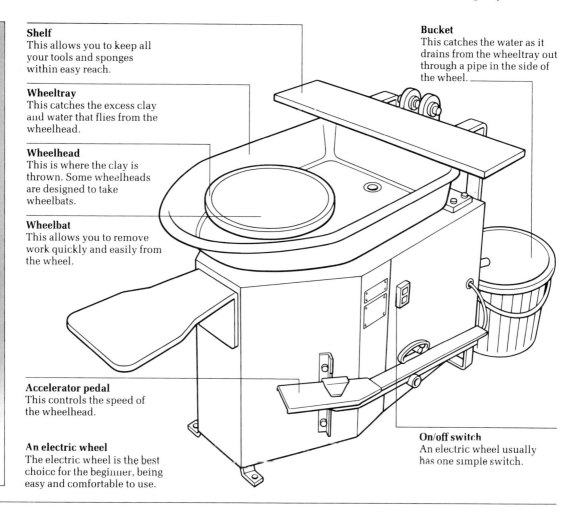

Shelf
This allows you to keep all your tools and sponges within easy reach.

Wheeltray
This catches the excess clay and water that flies from the wheelhead.

Wheelhead
This is where the clay is thrown. Some wheelheads are designed to take wheelbats.

Wheelbat
This allows you to remove work quickly and easily from the wheel.

Accelerator pedal
This controls the speed of the wheelhead.

An electric wheel
The electric wheel is the best choice for the beginner, being easy and comfortable to use.

Bucket
This catches the water as it drains from the wheeltray out through a pipe in the side of the wheel.

On/off switch
An electric wheel usually has one simple switch.

Setting up a home studio/3

useful and justifiable in a large studio, college or school, but are not essential. The only major pieces of equipment that are necessary are a kiln and a wheel.

All the necessary equipment can be bought from pottery suppliers. It is worth browsing through several suppliers' catalogues and comparing quality and prices before buying anything.

Kilns

Of all the pieces of equipment you will need, the kiln is the most essential. You can acquire everything else gradually. Most potters now use electric kilns, which are self-contained, fire cleanly and take up less space than kilns fired by solid fuel or gas. Electric kilns are relatively cheap to buy, although the operating, maintenance and repair costs are slightly higher than those of kilns fired by gas or solid fuel. When you buy a new kiln, all the necessary information will be supplied by the manufacturer. Instructions for operating and maintaining a kiln are given in detail in the firing section (see pp108-15).

Traditional electric kilns are loaded and unloaded from the front. More modern versions, however, can be loaded and unloaded from the top. These top-loading kilns are made from lightweight materials, are capable of firing up to 1300°C and range in size from 30 cubic litres to over 610 cubic litres. The smallest kilns can be operated from a normal electrical socket. For slightly larger kilns, up to 180-240 cubic litres in size, an electricity supply of 30-40 amps is needed. Do not buy a kiln that will obviously become too small for your eventual needs – 100 cubic litres is a realistic minimum size for the amateur potter.

Buying a second-hand electric kiln

Second-hand kilns are relatively cheap, but if you decide to buy one, make sure it is in good working order. Before you buy a second-hand electric kiln, check the manufacturer's plate. This tells you the maximum temperature to which the kiln should be fired, its cubic capacity, the required electrical supply and, most important of all, the phase of the wiring. All kilns should be installed by a qualified electrician unless they are small enough to operate from an ordinary electrical supply.

Wheels

An electric wheel is best for a beginner. This is far easier to use than a kickwheel, requires less physical effort, and allows large amounts of clay to be thrown with relative ease. A kickwheel is more difficult and tiring for the beginner to handle, especially the standing kickwheel, which can be uncomfortable if you are using it for long periods of time.

Any wheel you buy should be capable of coping with at least 10kg (22lb) of clay without incurring any loss of speed when pressure is applied to the rotating wheelhead; to check this, you should test any wheel you are thinking of buying by trying to slow the wheel with your hands when it is running at various speeds. It is also helpful to buy a wheelhead that takes removable wheelbats, on which pots can be thrown. Wheelbats are removable wooden discs that can be attached to any suitable wheelhead. You can throw a pot on the wheelbat as on an ordinary wheelhead and when you have finished, the whole wheelbat, with the pot still on it, can be removed simply and safely. It is worth buying as many wheelbats as you can afford, so that you can throw several pots in one working session without running out of them.

After you have taken these two considerations into account, the wheel you choose is a matter of personal preference; every wheel has its own idiosyncrasies, while every potter has his or her individual requirements. Some wheels slow down and stop as the accelerator is released; others will continue to rotate and only stop when the wheel is switched off. Some wheelheads are fixed; others can be rotated by hand when the motor is not operating.

The other option is to buy a second-hand wheel, but unless it is in very good condition, this may prove to be a false economy. If you do decide to buy a second-hand wheel, take somebody who is experienced and will view it objectively. Also check that the wheel runs smoothly, and that the framework does not show too many signs of wear – the overall appearance of a wheel usually indicates the state of its components.

Health and safety

A pottery studio is probably no more dangerous than the average kitchen, but it is important to be aware of the potential hazards, and know how to avoid accidents or health risks. Most safety precautions are common sense, but there are potential individual hazards that need special attention. If you have young children, you should make sure that they do not go into the studio unaccompanied and that any harmful substances are well out of reach.

Dust

The inevitable accumulation of dust in a pottery studio can be a major health problem. Silica is present in both clay and glazes, and if inhaled in large quantities over a long time, it may cause silicosis. Therefore, your studio and all your equipment should be regularly and thoroughly cleaned to reduce the build-up of dust. Before sweeping the floor, sprinkle water or wet sawdust over it; sweeping a dry floor only disperses the dust. Once swept, the floor should be mopped.

To reduce the risk of inhaling fine glaze dust, you should mix the powdered glaze with water before you sieve it, and wear a face mask while you are mixing it. If you intend to apply glaze by spraying (see pp120-1), you will also need the proprietary safety equipment, which you should use according to the manufacturer's instructions. These include an enclosed booth in which the work is sprayed and an extractor fan installed to remove the excess spray from the studio. You must also wear a respiratory mask while you are working.

Toxic materials

Most of the materials used in a pottery studio are harmful if swallowed, particularly any that contain cadmium, selenium, lithium, barium carbonate, borax, silica, flint, zinc oxide, antimony oxide, chromium oxide and nickel and copper compounds. Any containers holding any of these materials should be marked clearly as toxic and kept well out of the reach of any young children.

Even after firing, some materials are still toxic. Pottery decorated with certain low-fired glazes should not be used for storing or serving food or drink, for instance. This is because such glazes, if they contain lead, cadmium and copper, release toxic substances when the glaze comes into contact with a strong alkaline or acid material. Check glaze contents carefully. Manufacturers usually indicate which raw materials, ceramic colours or glazes are potentially dangerous. If you are ever in doubt about the safety of the pottery you are using for domestic purposes, you should ask an expert, or the manufacturer, for advice.

You should not eat, drink or smoke in the studio. Use scoops as much as possible when working with raw materials rather than handling them. If you cut or scratch yourself, wash the wound, apply some antiseptic, and cover it with a waterproof dressing.

Machinery

All machinery is dangerous if it is not used sensibly and according to the manufacturer's instructions. You should be particularly careful when using a pugmill and feeding clay into its hopper. Never use pieces of wood or metal to force the clay through the hopper, and keep the safety grille in position to prevent any possibility of catching your hands or clothing in the rotating mixer. Never wear dangling jewellery, ties, scarves or very loose or flapping clothes when operating any machinery.

The kiln

Manufacturers of kilns are obliged to comply with certain legal safety requirements so, provided that you install and operate your kiln strictly according to the manufacturer's instructions, you should never have any problems. However, before you actually install the kiln, check that its intended site is safe. Some buildings and work areas, particularly if they are made of wood, are simply too combustible to house any type or size of kiln. If you think there is any risk, you should have the building checked by an expert before the kiln is installed. You should also make sure that the floor is strong enough to take the weight of the kiln, and that there is a good clearance space around and above it.

The kiln itself should have door locks and interlocking switches, so that it is impossible to open the kiln door without switching off the electrical supply. It should also have a light to indicate whether or not the electricity is switched on.

To prevent any risk of fire, combustible materials should never be left on, or close to, a kiln during firing. For example, do not put work which is still standing on wooden bats to dry on the kiln.

You must take great care when firing is in progress. If the kiln cannot be housed in a separate room, it should be contained in such a way that prevents any danger of someone accidentally touching it and burning themselves. Do not look through the spyholes with the naked eye when firing is in progress, as this can be harmful. If you are ever uncertain about how hot the outer casing of the kiln is, try the spittle test. Place a few drops of water or spittle on the casing; if it sizzles, the kiln is still hot. Before you load or unload the kiln, or before any repair or maintenance work is carried out, you should always switch the kiln off at the mains isolation point, rather than just turning the kiln off at the control switch.

All kilns give off unpleasant, and potentially toxic, vapours during firing, so it is important that the kiln area is well-ventilated. Keep windows and doors open if possible. If the kiln is in a very enclosed and badly-ventilated place, an extractor fan should be fitted above it – this will dispose of both the fumes and the excess heat produced.

In the event of an electric kiln starting a fire, do not try to put it out with water; use a proprietary electrical fire extinguisher (it is worth keeping one of these in the studio near the kiln). A fire from an electric kiln is probably due to faulty or old wiring. Usually, in the case of a fire, the fuse will blow, isolating the power supply, so the fire should be short-lived, provided that there is nothing near the fire to fuel it further.

If a fire occurs, or a fault is apparent in the kiln, leave the kiln to cool. You should have it checked by an electrician, or the kiln manufacturer, as soon as possible, and should not use it again until such a check has been completed.

Tools and accessories

When you begin pottery, you only need a few basic pieces of equipment. Other items can be bought as you need them. For general use you need buckets, bowls, small containers, measuring jugs, funnels and a range of brushes. A whirler – a rotating work base – is also useful.

For weighing clay, you need scales that can take a minimum of 5kg (11lb); plastic bowls to hold water while you are working at the wheel; several sponges, ranging from a large one to mop water from the wheel to a small one on a stick for removing water from the insides of thrown pots; plastic buckets to catch waste clay and water as it drains from the wheel; needles or pins for trimming; rubber and metal kidneys for smoothing your work; cutting wires for removing pots from the wheel; measuring calipers; and scrapers for removing clay from surfaces. You will need a potter's harp for cutting clay; a potter's knife; trimming tools; a rolling pin and wooden rails for making slabs (see p60); and hessian on which to roll slabs.

For decorating and glazing you will need stiff card, tracing paper and scissors; slip trailers; large plastic bottles for storing slip; scales for weighing small amounts of material – up to 50g (3½oz); wire pottery sieves of 60, 100 and 120 mesh; a lawn brush; a mortar and pestle; and a lawn cup.

Hand-forming and decoration
The tools shown here are all readily available from pottery suppliers. When buying tools, it is worth looking at several suppliers' catalogues to compare both the prices and the quality.

Sieve (1); hessian (2); slip trailers (3); calipers (4); whirler (5); mortar and pestle (6); rolling pin (7); wooden strip guides (8); pottery knife (9); slip or lawn brush (10); rubber kidneys (11); cutting wire (12); steel scrapers (13); potter's harp (14). ▷

Brushes
A lawn or slip brush (1) is used for applying slip or glaze in large quantities. It can also be used for passing powdered materials through sieves. Cut liner brushes (2) and squirrel-hair brushes (3) are used for more detailed decorative work. ◁

Turning and modelling
Both turning tools (1) and stem turning tools (2) are used to trim thrown pots. Looped modelling tools (3) are used for hollowing clay and sculpture; boxwood modelling tools (4) are for carving, sculpting and texturing plastic clay. ▽

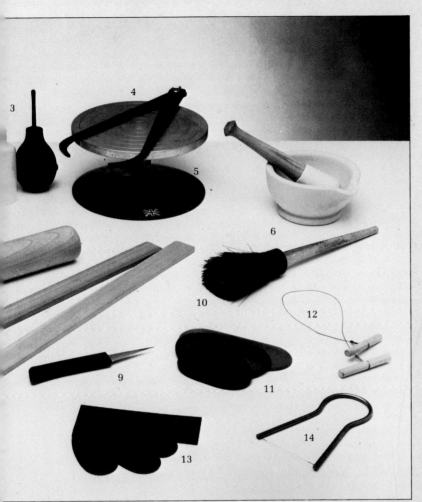

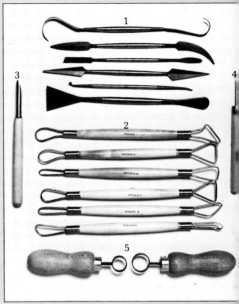

Clay working tools

Double-ended forged steel modelling tools (1) are mainly used for carving and texturing leatherhard clay and plaster. Ground modelling tools (2) are suitable for delicate modelling work. A hole-cutter (3) and needle (4) for trimming are essential. Coilers (5) provide an alternative to rolling coils by hand. △

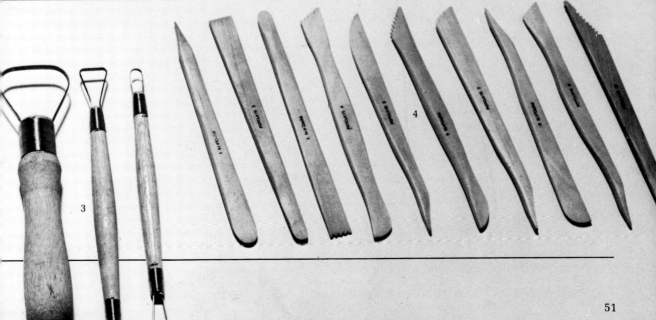

Experimenting with local clay

Finding and working with local clay provides the perfect introduction to pottery. Even if you do not feel like spending hours up to your waist in mud, making and firing work of this kind is still worthwhile.

As this type of clay can be fired at a much lower temperature than most clays, objects made from local clay are ideal for trying out simple sawdust kilns, which only reach temperatures of between 550-600°C Although pottery fired in a sawdust kiln tends to be somewhat brittle, the work you produce should still be perfectly satisfactory.

Recognizing local clay

Local clay is easy to find – you may well find some in your back garden. Building sites, old brick works and river banks are also likely sources. It is recognizable by being plastic. This means that when moist and gently compressed, it holds firmly together.

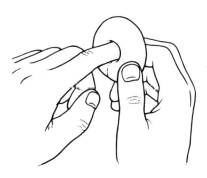

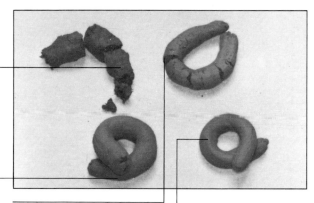

1 This material is not clay; the particles do not hold together.

2 This material only has a minimum clay content and is also unsuitable.

3 This has a reasonable clay content, but the cracks indicate a rather coarse, 'short' clay.

4 This is the type of local clay you need, being plastic and quite clean.

Testing for plasticity
Pick up a small handful of earth, roll it into a sausage and bend it into a hoop. Note how this material behaves.

Some ideas to try

Make a group of animals, using spheres made from two pinch pots (see pp54-5) as a basis for the animals' bodies. Create the impression of fur, skin, feathers or spines by texturing the clay surface with different objets trouvés – combs, pens and pencils, screws, chains, pieces of bark and twigs, wire mesh and pins are just a few possibilities.

Local clay can be used for almost any type of pottery, provided that it is well cleaned and prepared (see pp40-3). Try some of the following suggestions, or adapt them for your own individual experiments to use as an introduction to working with clay.

Cut out the profiles of some animals, birds or fishes from a flat sheet of clay. Add their features by pressing small pellets, coils and strips of clay into the surface.

Make a rounded pinch pot. When it is leatherhard, polish its surface by carefully rubbing it with a smooth tool, the back of a spoon, or even your finger, until it becomes glossy. This polishing technique is known as burnishing.

Allow your work to dry thoroughly. You should leave the pots in a warm place for at least three days before firing. All these objects can be fired in a normal kiln, provided that the temperature does not exceed 1000°C. Alternatively they can be fired in a sawdust kiln.

Building a sawdust kiln
This can be built by a complete novice in under 15 minutes from 28 house bricks, a metal dustbin lid or four paving slabs and a metal sheet, a concrete slab, plus enough fine sawdust to fill the entire kiln. Construct it outside, where it can be safely left. A sawdust kiln can also be made from a perforated dustbin. The pottery it produces is black in colour – this can be enhanced by rubbing it with boot polish. Sawdust kilns are not failsafe, as the heat is unevenly distributed, causing the clay to heat and contract at different rates, so some work may break.

Build a brick chimney, two bricks by two bricks square and three bricks high. Then, place the remaining four bricks across each corner of the opening at the top, leaving a small gap between each brick. Check that the dustbin lid fits comfortably over the top of the chimney.

When your work is completely dry, put approximately 7cm (2¾in) of sawdust in the bottom of the kiln. Then put three or four pieces of pottery in the sawdust, making sure that there is at least 3cm (1⅛in) of sawdust between them. Cover these pieces with another 7cm (2¾in) of sawdust and add another layer of pottery. Fill the whole kiln in this way, and finish with a thick layer of sawdust on top.

Place one or two sheets of crumpled newspaper on top of the sawdust and set light to them. Once the newspaper has burnt, the flames will die, but the sawdust will continue to smoulder gently. Now put the lid on the top of the chimney. The kiln is perfectly safe and so can be left for the necessary 10 to 15 hours. There may not be much smoke but the sawdust will continue to smoulder.

The sawdust will burn away to leave your work at the bottom of the kiln. Wash the pottery to remove the burnt sawdust.

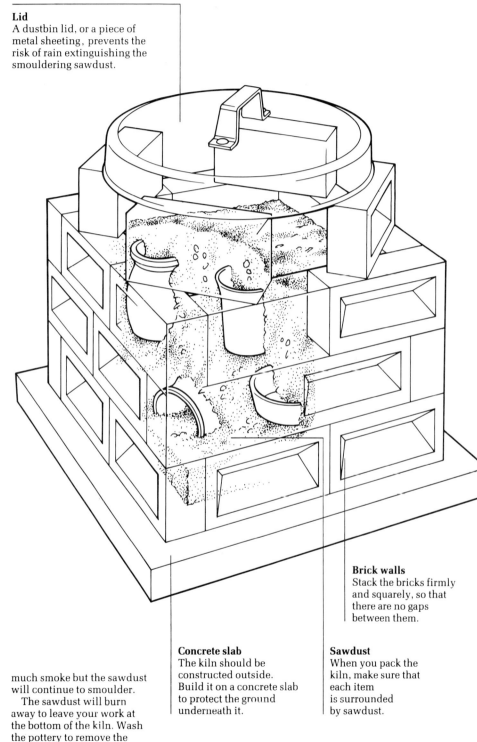

Lid
A dustbin lid, or a piece of metal sheeting, prevents the risk of rain extinguishing the smouldering sawdust.

Brick walls
Stack the bricks firmly and squarely, so that there are no gaps between them.

Concrete slab
The kiln should be constructed outside. Build it on a concrete slab to protect the ground underneath it.

Sawdust
When you pack the kiln, make sure that each item is surrounded by sawdust.

Pinching

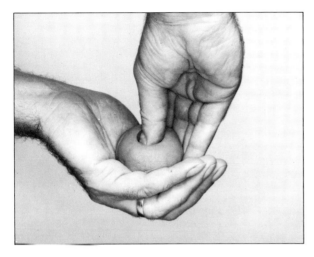

Pinching is the easiest and most straightforward forming technique and provides a good opportunity for you to become used to working with clay. Almost any clay is suitable for pinching, providing that it is plastic enough to be worked without cracking. Simple pinch pots can be used to make egg cups, dishes and vases. You can also join several pinch pots together with stiff slurry to make, for example, candelabra and cacti gardens.

Making a pinch pot

1 Take a small ball of prepared plastic clay firmly but gently in your left hand. Push your right thumb into the centre of the clay until it almost reaches the bottom of the ball. Place your right-hand fingers around the outside of the ball, and, rotating it slowly, squeeze the clay gently and rhythmically until a pot begins to take shape.

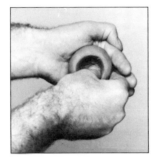

2 You will find the walls are thin at the bottom, but thicker at the top. To thin the upper sections of the walls, move your right thumb into a higher position and then continue rotating and squeezing the clay. ▷

3 Continue this process until the walls of the pot are of an even thickness throughout. It is almost inevitable that the rim will be uneven, but you can trim it with a pin if you wish.

Adding feet

You can easily add a foot to any pinched form. To do this, cut a thin strip from a rolled clay sheet (see p60), which is just long enough to form a circle to fit to the base.

Score the base of the pot and the edge of the clay strip. Bend the clay strip to form a circle and join both ends with a little slurry. Fix the foot to the base with a little slurry. Smooth the join with a damp sponge.

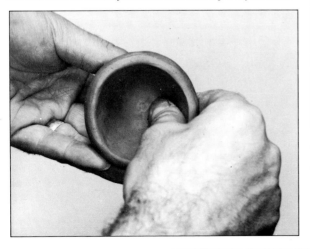

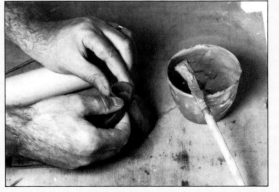

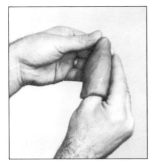

Making a tall thin pot

1 Place your thumb in the clay as before, but this time squeeze the clay around your thumb with your left hand. This will force the clay to move upwards. △

2 A slender foot can be made by rolling the base of the pot gently along the edge of a table. ▷

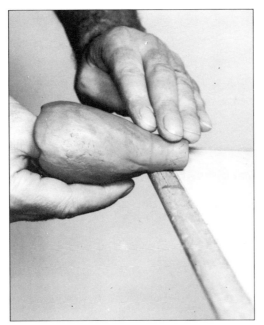

3 To make the base more stable, hollow it out from underneath with a loop of wire, to form a foot. ▽

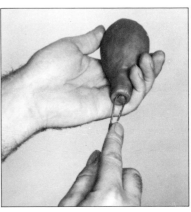

Making a sphere from two pinch pots

Make two basic pinch pots of equal size. Tap the rims of both pots against a flat surface until they are completely level. Score both rims well with a knife and apply a thick coating of slurry to each. Press the rims together firmly, twisting them slightly as they make contact to ensure a good bond. Smooth the join with a damp sponge until it is *invisible. Pierce a hole in the sphere before firing.*

Large spheres can be made but will need some support from the inside. You should therefore pack both halves with crumpled newspaper before joining them. This will burn away during firing.

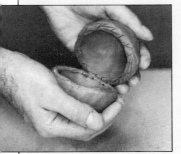

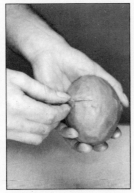

Experimenting with pinching
Make your own group of different, but related, pinch pots. Try making both bulbous and long thin shapes, using flared and narrowed rims.

Coiling

This technique of building forms from rings or spirals of rolled clay can be used to create many different types of hollow clay forms, including sculptures. Use a smooth, plastic clay for small pots or shapes and a coarser, open-bodied clay for larger forms. However, whatever type of clay you use, the clay should always be plastic enough for you to form the coils easily.

Coils can be hand-rolled, as here, or they can be machine-made by an extruder. It is vital that the coils you use are of an even thickness throughout, or, in turn, your work will be uneven. Roll out enough clay for at least one complete layer of the form you are making to ensure an even structure. Keep the coils in polythene until you are ready to use them.

Rolling coils
Form a rough coil of clay between your hands and roll this evenly forwards and backwards with flattened palms. Work from the centre of the coil, moving your hands outwards and away from each other. If the coil becomes flat, stop and pat it into a round shape before resuming rolling. ▷

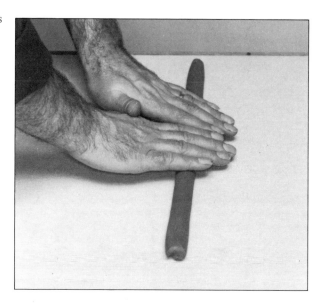

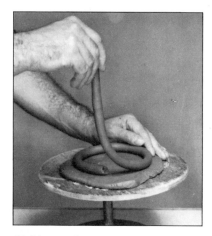

Making a coil pot
1 Cover a board with newspaper. Press out a piece of clay into a flat disc to form the base. Prepare some coils. These must be approximately as thick as the base, and long enough to fit around its whole circumference.

Place the first coil around the inside edge of the base. Cut the ends and press them together to make a snug join. Support the outside of the coil and base with your left hand, and, with the index finger or thumb of your right hand, pull the top of the coil down and blend it into the base from the inside until the join between coil and base is invisible.

2 Place a second coil on top of the first but make sure that the ends do not meet over the join of the first coil. Using your left hand as a support, pull the top of the second coil downwards

from the inside as before. Smooth down the join. Never squeeze the coils when you join them to the existing clay wall as this will make the form expand and eventually distort.

3 To build a straight-sided pot, repeat this process until the walls are the required height. If you do not want the coiled effect to be visible on the outside, smooth the clay down before it dries. Trim the base with a knife.

Ovoid coil pot by Ruth Duckworth
Coil pots can be made to swell or narrow as you require. To widen a coil pot, place each coil slightly on the outside of the one beneath as you construct it. To narrow the shape, place each coil slightly on the inside of the one beneath it. The pot here shows the freedom of shape and form the coiling technique allows.

Making a large coil pot

Use a well-grogged, open-bodied clay for building large coil pots. Add only a few layers at a time and, to ensure that the pot is stable, allow them to stiffen slightly before continuing. For extra stability, you can pack the pot with balls of newspaper.

Whenever you have to stop working, leave the bottom coils uncovered to dry, but keep the top three or four coils damp by covering them with polythene. Your work will keep like this for one or two days, provided that it is not in a hot atmosphere. If you leave your work for longer, cover it totally with polythene. When you recommence work, score the top coil of the pot and coat it with slurry before you add a new coil to ensure a good join. Allow the pot to dry thoroughly before firing.

To make a symmetrical coil pot, draw the profile of the pot on a sheet of stiff card to the required size. Construct your pot so that its outline conforms to this profile. This is done by holding the template against the sides of the pot to make sure that the shape is developing correctly.

The large coil pot shown (right) was made by Adrian Glew (student).

Making a coil jar with a former

Coil pots can be moulded around a 'former', a type of mould that supports and shapes the work during construction. The following items are useful formers: square, rectangular and round sections of wood; boxes of any material; cardboard and plastic tubes; plastic bowls and buckets; and even dustbin lids. However, if their surfaces are non-porous, the formers should be covered with newspaper before you begin work to prevent the clay sticking.

If you are fitting coils around the outside of a former, remove it before the clay dries and contracts, as your work will otherwise crack. However, if you fit the coils around the inside of a former, this is not necessary as the coils contract away from it as they dry.

Making a jar

1 Line the inside of a plastic bowl with dampened – but not wet – strips of newspaper. These will prevent the clay coils from sticking to the former.

Place a flat even disc of clay inside the bowl. This forms the base of the jar. ▷

2 Place the first coil on the base, making sure it is in contact with the surface of the bowl throughout its length. Fit the ends of the coil together in a snug join, and smooth the first coil into the base with your fingers. △

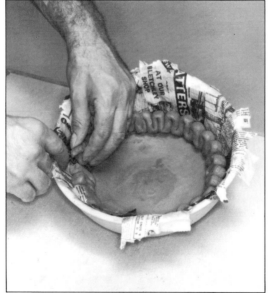

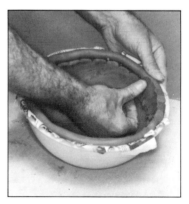

4 Fix the third coil in place, and blend it into the second layer as before. The fourth layer can be composed of compact coiled clay circles, made from equal lengths of coil. Fit each circle snugly in place against the previous layer. Smooth each into the clay wall. △

3 As you add the next layer, bend the coil into tight closed waves. Make sure again that the coil fits snugly against the bowl and the previous layer. Smooth the coil into the previous layer, checking that all the joins are invisible. △

5 Continue adding coil layers until you reach the top of the bowl. Pack the form with crumpled newspaper and place a board over the rim. △

6 Holding both firmly, invert the bowl and board so that the board is underneath. Peel away the newspaper from the surface of the pot. Cut a hole in the base of the coiled form, large enough to admit your hand. You have now completed the top half of the jar. Using the same bowl, make another coiled form as before. You can follow the same pattern of coil layers that you used for the first half of the jar or use a different design. ◁

7 When you have finished the second half of the jar, pack the inside with plenty of newspaper for support. Take the top half of the jar and join the two rim to rim. Cut a hole in the top, place your hand inside the jar and smooth the join from the inside with your thumb or index finger. Carefully draw out the newspaper from the jar. ▷

8 Fix more coils around the top rim of the jar. These may be smoothed into the rim on both the inside and outside of the jar or on the inside only. ▷

9 The jar can be made into an attractive lampstand. To do this, narrow the neck until it is no more than 6-7cm (2⅖ 2¾in) in diameter to admit a bulb fitting, and pierce a small hole near the base for the cable. △

Slabbing

This is the technique of rolling sheets or slabs of clay. The slabs can be used in various ways. You can cut them to make tiles or plaques, wrap them around formers to make pots and vases, or fit cut slabs together to construct sculptures.

You can cut several slabs at once from a block of clay or roll each individually – both methods are shown here. When rolling slabs, work on hessian to prevent them sticking to the work surface. The slabs should be rolled between two wooden guides, both between 1.2cm (½in) and 2.4cm (1in) thick. This ensures that the slab is of an even thickness throughout. Use a coarse clay for large work – crank mixes and raku clays are suitable types – but use a more plastic clay for small or wrapped forms.

The fabric on which the slab is rolled will texture the surface. If you do not like this effect, keep the textured side on the inside of any form you make with the slab.

Cutting slabs from a clay block
To make several slabs quickly, cut through a clay block shaped to the required size with a potter's harp. Move the harp wire up a notch with each cut to slice the next slab.

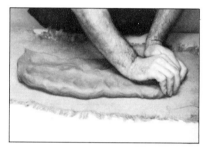

Hand rolling slabs
1 Place the clay on the hessian between the guides, and press it out with the palms of your hands. Turn the clay regularly, peeling it carefully from the hessian each time. △

2 When the slab is roughly the right thickness, roll it smooth with a heavy rolling pin, working from the centre of the sheet outwards. Score any air pockets that may form with a pin.

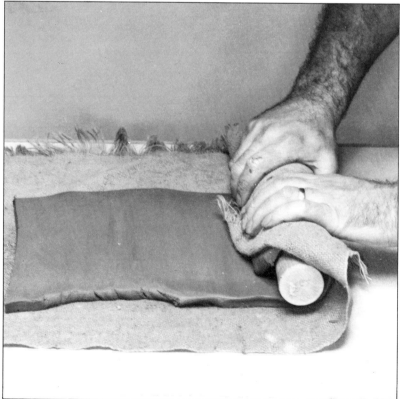

3 Turn the slab regularly. To avoid tearing it, wrap both the clay and the hessian round the pin – like a swiss roll – turn the rolling pin over and unroll the slab on to a new sheet of hessian, with the old hessian facing upwards. Peel away the old hessian and continue rolling.

Tiles and plaques

Tiles and plaques can easily be cut from a prepared slab. They are prone to warp, especially when the clay is drying. This can be avoided by ensuring that the sheet of clay you use is well grogged and between 1.2cm (½in) and 2.4cm (1in) thick, and of an even thickness throughout. Add any surface decoration before the plaque or tiles are cut from the sheet so you do not distort them. Dry them slowly and thoroughly, turning them regularly.

Making a set of tiles

1 Draw templates for the plaque or tiles on card, and cut them out (see pp34-7). Place the templates on a prepared clay sheet, and draw lightly round them with a pointed tool. Several tiles can be drawn at once, but allow a little space around each one. ◁

2 Remove the templates and decorate the surface of each tile, if you wish. Try impressing (see pp130-1), incising (see p132) or inlaying (see pp134-5) a design in the surface.

3 Place the templates in position again and redraw the outlines of each tile accurately. Then carefully cut out the tiles with a sharp knife. Smooth down all the edges of the tiles gently with a damp sponge.

4 Just before the tiles become leatherhard, gouge out thin channels of clay from the undersides. This will help the tiles to dry evenly and thoroughly. ▷

5 Chamfer the bottom edges of the tiles with a knife and sponge them smooth. If you are fitting a number of tiles together, chamfering both top and bottom edges gives a clean finish. However, you should not chamfer the top edges if the surface decoration runs continuously across several tiles as this will spoil the design. ▷

Project – making a door plaque

You can easily design and make a number or name plate for the door of your house, or a friend's, simply by mounting the appropriate lettering or numbering and edging cut from clay on a plaque. Study various types of lettering to see which appeals to you. Remember that it is important that the lettering you choose is clear and easy to read.

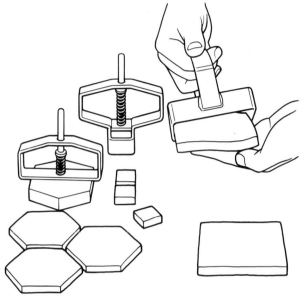

Making a door plaque

1 Make a template for your plaque and trace all of the outlines *(see pp34-7)* on to a 1.2-cm (½-in) clay slab. Trace the outlines of your lettering, or numbering, and the edging on to a separate clay slab. △

Tile cutters
Tile cutters speed up the process of cutting tiles and can be bought in various shapes and sizes from most pottery suppliers. △

2 Cut out the plaque, lettering and edging. Mark the positions of the edging and lettering on the plaque and score the areas to which they will be attached. Place the edging and the lettering on the plaque to make sure they fit, then fix them in place with stiff slurry. △

3 Smooth down the joins and edges with a damp sponge. Before the clay becomes leatherhard, bore holes in either side of the plaque, making them large enough to take screws. Leave the plaque to dry on a flat surface away from draughts or direct heat. △

Project – making a dish

Free shallow forms, made from clay slabs, are extremely easy to make. You can produce a large plate or dish, which makes a marvellous serving platter, with very little effort, simply by shaping a circle cut from a sheet of clay over a former. Such simple dishes, with their smooth open surfaces, offer perfect opportunities for experimenting with decoration. Before you begin work, cover your work surface with newspaper to prevent the clay slab from sticking.

1 Make a circle from a thick coil of clay and cover it with a smooth layer of dampened newspaper strips. Cut a circle from a clay slab slightly wider in diameter than the coil. ◁

2 Place the clay circle over the coil. Work over the centre of the clay circle with a damp sponge, moving around the inside of the coil to define the line between the base and rim of the dish. ▷

Creating a landscape

Large shallow slab forms can be textured and decorated in low relief to create a landscape effect. This makes a marvellous decorative plaque or dish. Take a large slab of clay and cut a gently curving shape from it. Tuck crumpled balls of newspaper of various sizes underneath the slab to form the hills and valleys of an undulating landscape. Incise (see pp132-3), impress (see p130), and apply (see p135) decoration, as you wish.

3 Smooth the rim and edges of the dish with the sponge to create a good finish. Leave the dish to dry. Remove the coil just before firing – if it is removed earlier the dish may sag. The paper will come away with the coil. ▽

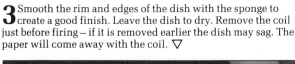

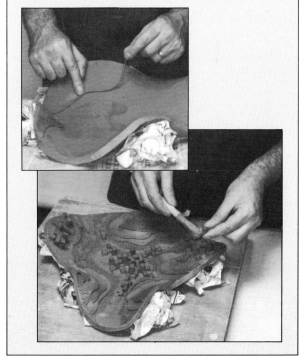

Folded slab forms

Pliable sheets of clay can be wrapped around formers to make vases and pots of many shapes and sizes. Making a vase using a rolling pin as a former is an ideal starting point for your own experiments. Formers should be straight-sided and should be covered with newspaper so that they can be removed without damaging the form itself. Cardboard tubing, different-sized pieces of wood, boxes and bricks are all ideal.

Making a rolling-pin vase

1 Prepare a sheet of clay long enough to wrap comfortably around the rolling pin. Cut straight edges along the sides of the slab. Lay the rolling pin along the edge of one end. △

2 Wrap the clay firmly around the rolling pin. When it has completed one revolution and the edge of the slab meets clay again, mark a line. Cut along the line to remove the excess clay. ▷

3 Chamfer both vertical edges to 45° so that they lie parallel and fit together snugly. Score both edges well and fix them together with a thick coating of slurry. Smooth the join with a sponge. △

4 Stand the rolling pin on another piece of clay slab (preferably an offcut from your original slab to ensure the base and sides have the same consistency). Draw around the bottom of the vase to mark out the base. Remove the vase, and cut out the base with a sharp knife. Score the base and bottom edges of the vase. Join them firmly together with thick slurry. Trim around the base. ▷

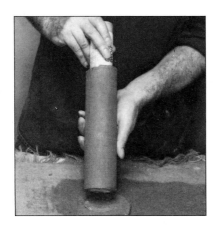

5 Having decided the height of your vase, mark the line of the top edge accurately all the way round the cylinder. Cut along the line with a knife. If you wish, you can add another thin strip of clay around the rim to thicken it. Sponge the edges and joins smooth. ▷

Making a winged vase

1 As for the previous vase, use a rolling pin as a former. Draw a template *(see pp34-7)* for the wings on tracing paper. This should have one straight side and one curved side. Using the template, cut two wings from a sheet of clay. They should be no longer than the rolling pin. Place the rolling pin 2.4cm (1in) in from the straight edge of one wing. △

2 Place the second wing over the rolling pin, facing outwards in the opposite direction to the first. Adjust both wings until they snugly enclose the pin. △

3 Score the edges of both wings, and fix them firmly and snugly in place around the pin. Supporting the vase with both hands, turn it upright. Smooth down all the joins. Mark out the base and attach it as you did the base of the rolling pin vase *(opposite).* ◁

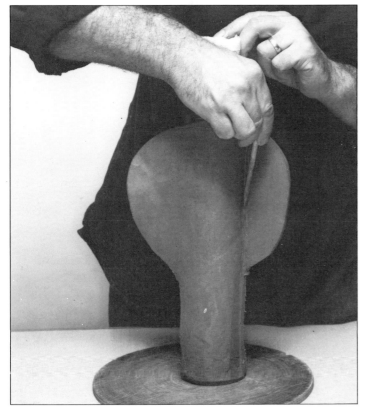

4 Pierce holes carefully in the wings with a pin. Trim the rim and base and smooth the vase with a sponge. Take care not to damage or tear the wings as you smooth them. △

Slab construction

Slabs can be cut and then assembled when they are soft-leatherhard (just pliable), to construct a great variety of exciting forms – you can make architectural constructions of buildings and bridges, or gently mould the slabs to make vases and even jugs. It is vital that the slab sections are of the same thickness throughout and that they are precisely measured and cut.

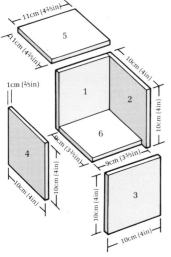

Making a cube

1 This is a good introduction to the technique of slab construction, as it is a good exercise in precision cutting and construction. Cut the four sides for the cube (1, 2, 3, 4), the top, (5), and the base (6) from a 1-cm (²⁄₅-in) thick clay slab. When the tiles are soft-leatherhard, place the base (6) on a workboard covered with newspaper. Score its four edges. ◁

2 Mark and then score a 1-cm (²⁄₅-in) strip along one edge of one side (1). Apply slurry to one edge of the base (6), and join the side (1) securely to this edge, so that it is flush with one end of the base but overhangs the other end by 1cm (²⁄₅-in). Press a thin coil of clay along the join to strengthen it.

3 Score 1-cm (²⁄₅-in) strips along the bottom and one side of the next tile (2). Paint these strips with slurry and attach the tile to the first side (1) and the base (6). Strengthen the joins with thin coils of clay. △

4 Attach the remaining two sides, (3 *and* 4) in the same way. As you progress, make sure that each is fixed firmly in place and each join is exactly square. ▷

5 Score the top open edges of the sides (1, 2, 3 and 4). Score 1-cm (²⁄₅-in) strips around all four edges of the top (5) and fix it firmly in place with slurry. Pierce a small escape hole for air in the base of the cube.

6 When the cube is leatherhard, chamfer the edges with a sharp knife, and gently and carefully smooth both the joints and edges with a barely-damp sponge.

Making a slab vase

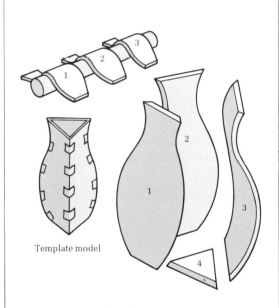

Template model

Measure accurately and cut cardboard templates (see pp34-7) for the sides (1, 2, 3) and base (4) of the vase. Make a model of the vase from the templates to check its construction. Cut the sides (1, 2, 3) and base (4) from a slab. Chamfer the edges of the three sides (1, 2, 3) and the base (4) to 30°. Bend each side into its curved shape. Support them over a round surface as they dry, so they do not lose their shape. Score the edges of the sides (1, 2, 3) and join them with slurry. Fix the base in place in the same way.

Slab sculpture by Dave Edmonds
This potter's work shows the great potential of slab construction and displays wonderful ingenuity. He is greatly influenced by architectural forms and early Chinese ceramics.

Modelling with clay

Any type of clay can be used for modelling and sculpture. However, if you intend to make large-scale sculptures, you should use coarser types of clay or add grog or sand to a more plastic clay. To establish the correct proportion for a figure, use the length of the head as a measuring unit. The average adult measures about eight head lengths in height; the torso measures about three lengths; the legs measure about four lengths; and the arms measure about three lengths.

Modelling clay figures

1 First shape the head. Make three clay coils – one as thick as the head for the legs, the second half as thick for the arms and the third twice as wide for the torso. ▷

2 Attach the limbs to the body with stiff slurry. Make several figures in this way and gently form them into different positions. You will usually find that the most stable are those where the figure is sitting, kneeling, squatting or on all fours; standing figures are usually the most unstable. Use pieces of clay to support the body. Insert paper between the supports and figures to keep them separated until they dry. You can also explore the possibilities of using two figures together. ▷

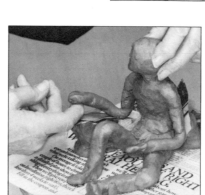

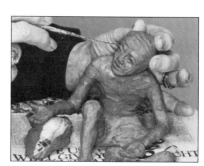

3 When you are satisfied with the overall shape, add details and features with a modelling tool.

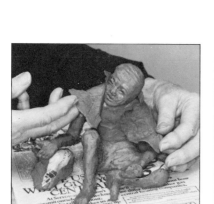

4 The figure can be clothed by pressing out thin sheets of clay to the required size and draping or folding them around the body.

5 Make a group of figures; use their expressions and posture to establish a relationship between them. ▷

Solid sculptures

1 Solid sculptures must be hollowed after they have been completed to ensure that they do not break during firing – a clay form will dry and fire unevenly if it is too thick. Ideally the walls of the form should be no thicker than 2.5cm (1in).

Cover your work surface with newspaper to prevent the clay sticking to it. Mark the outline of your sculpture in a block of prepared clay cut to approximately the size of your intended sculpture. With a pottery knife, cut around the main outlines. ▷

2 Carefully carve out the recessed areas of the sculpture with a looped modelling tool. Cut away any other extraneous clay.

3 When you have finished the basic outline, carefully model the details. If you need to add any clay, slap it on forcefully so that no air becomes trapped.

4 Clarify the lines of the sculpture with a fine modelling tool. Add any necessary surface textures and smooth any rough edges.

Coiled sculptures

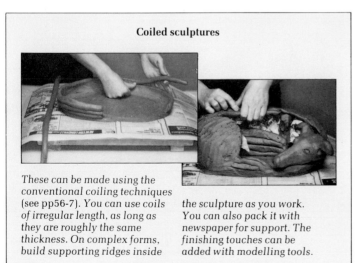

These can be made using the conventional coiling techniques (see pp56-7). You can use coils of irregular length, as long as they are roughly the same thickness. On complex forms, build supporting ridges inside the sculpture as you work. You can also pack it with newspaper for support. The finishing touches can be added with modelling tools.

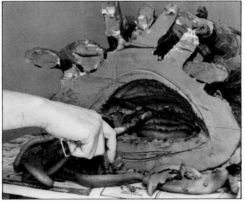

5 Before the clay has dried to leatherhard, hollow the sculpture out from beneath. Support it at one side with a cushion of crushed newspaper, taking great care not to damage it.

Making moulds

Moulds are used as formers to shape clay and are usually made from plaster of Paris. The simplest type to make is a drop mould. A second type of mould, known as a drape or hump mould, can also be made from this. To work successfully, the moulds must slope outwards from their bases and be free of undercuts.

To mix the plaster for the mould, gradually sprinkle powdered plaster of Paris into a bucket of water, stirring the mixture continually until it begins to thicken. The plaster is now ready for use but it must be used immediately as it sets quickly.

If clay becomes contaminated with plaster, it will be ruined. For this reason, when using plaster you should not work in the same area in which you prepare, store or form clay.

Making a drop mould

1 Cut out a template (see p57) in the shape of the mould and, using this, build a clay model. The model shown here will make a mould for a rectangular tray.

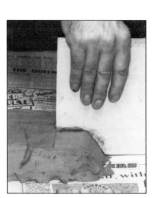

2 Check the shape of the mould model with a profile template. Check that there are no undercuts in which the plaster will become trapped, as this will prevent the easy removal of the model. ▷

3 Make a frame around the model with four wooden boards or a clay wall, sealing any joints with clay. The frame should allow for a 5-cm (2-in) gap around the model and be 5cm (2in) or so deeper than the model.

4 Pour the prepared plaster into one corner of the frame, allowing it to rise over the model until the frame is filled completely. Pour the plaster slowly to prevent any air being trapped between the model and the plaster.

5 Allow the plaster to set firm and then remove the frame. Invert the plaster block and carefully remove the clay model inside it. Leave the mould for a week to dry thoroughly.

Making a drape or hump mould
1 Carefully coat the inside surface of a drop mould with a

proprietary releasing agent, such as soft soap – this is available from pottery suppliers.

2 Place a clay coil around the outside edge of the drop mould to prevent any spillage. Pour plaster carefully into the drop mould. Before it sets firm, press a section of cardboard tubing into the surface. This acts as a stand for the completed drape mould. △

3 When the plaster is hard, lift out the drape mould from the drop mould. If they do not part easily, immerse both totally in water. ▷

Using moulds

The simplest moulded forms can be made by rolling a slab of clay *(see p60)* and then pressing this over or into your chosen mould. This technique is known as press-moulding. It is best, initially, to practise press-moulding from fairly straightforward moulds, such as the ones shown here. Press-moulded forms can be joined together with slurry and you will find that, even with three or four very basic moulds, you will be able to create a variety of interesting forms.

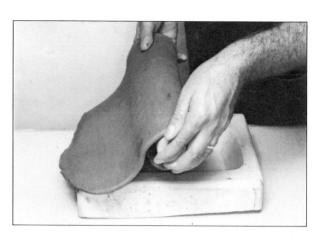

Using a drop mould

1 Roll an even slab of clay that is large enough to cover the surface of the mould comfortably. Lift the sheet on to the mould, wrapping it round a rolling pin first to prevent it breaking. Smooth the clay into the mould with a sponge. ▷

2 Trim away the excess clay around the rim of the mould with a taut cutting wire. Draw the wire from the centre of the mould out to each end in turn, keeping it flush with the top of the mould. This will prevent the clay lifting. ▷

3 Smooth the clay again thoroughly with a damp sponge and a plastic kidney. Then leave it to dry until it can be safely removed without the risk of damage or distortion. ▷

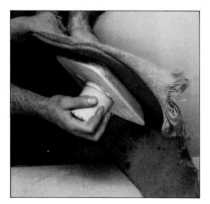

Using a drape mould

1 Place the mould face down on a sheet of clay. Holding the sheet against the mould, turn them both over in one swift movement. △

2 Smooth the clay with a damp sponge so that it fits closely against the mould. Trim away the excess clay with a pottery knife or a potter's harp. Allow the clay to stiffen before you remove it from the mould. ◁

Creative press-moulding
All the examples shown here were made by joining simple moulded forms together. Each of the bottles were made by joining two moulded dishes rim to rim and then adding thrown necks. The tall sculptural piece (centre) was made from a drop mould, which used a football as a model; a thrown stem was then attached. ◁

Drape mould decoration

Cut some shapes from a sheet of soft-leatherhard clay. The clay can either be the same colour as the sheet you will use for the body of the press-moulded form, or a different colour. Arrange the shapes to create an exciting design, and position them carefully on the mould's surface.

Lay a sheet of soft, plastic clay over the mould and smooth it down with a damp sponge. When you turn out the clay form from the mould, you will find that the clay shapes are embedded in the surface to create an attractive decorative effect.

Drop mould decoration

Press strips and pellets of plastic clay into the mould and smooth them together with a damp sponge. Richly-decorative surface textures can be produced in this way on press-moulded forms.

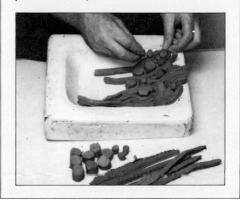

Learning to throw

Everyone longs to be able to produce pots at the wheel with the dexterity of a master potter. Mastering the basic technique of throwing is one of the most exciting facets of the craft, but it is not the easiest of skills to acquire. However, although using a wheel properly requires considerable practice, its mastery is well within everyone's reach.

Which clay to use

It is important to use the right clay for throwing, and to prepare it properly. Throwing clay must be soft, plastic and sensitive enough to enable you to shape it quickly and easily and, at the same time, rigid enough to retain its shape while wet.

For these reasons, it is better to buy specially prepared throwing clay from a supplier than to mix your own. However, although the clay should be supplied ready for use, you should still ensure that it is well prepared by wedging and kneading it thoroughly (see p42-3) to eliminate air pockets and inconsistencies. Always try to prepare enough clay to last for an entire work session – in the long run, you will find that this will save you time and trouble.

Preparing to throw

Throwing techniques are basically the same, regardless of whether you are using a kick or electric wheel. An

Sitting at the wheel

There is no one correct position but it is important that your working position is comfortable. ▽

electric wheel is better for a beginner, since it is easier to use and so lets you concentrate completely on throwing rather than on operating the wheel.

Before you start work, you will need the following items close to hand: a good-sized bowl of water; a sponge; a needle; turning tools (see p50); cutting wire; tiles or boards on which to place the thrown work if you are not using removable wheelbats. Your prepared clay should be cut up into pieces, each weighing about 0.75kg (1½lb), and then slapped into well-rounded balls. Wrap the balls you do not intend to use immediately in polythene. This prevents the clay from drying out and hardening.

Working at the wheel

It is important that your working position is comfortable, stable, and gives you the maximum access to the wheel itself. If your wheel has a seat, ensure that it slopes gently towards the wheelhead. Check that you can lean over the centre of the wheelhead easily. It is a

Centring

1 Place the clay ball firmly in the centre of the wheelhead. If you miss the centre, drag the clay with both hands as near to it as you can. Slowly rotate the wheelhead by hand, gently patting the clay into a dome as it turns. △

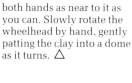

2 Start the wheel, setting its speed at about three-quarters of maximum. Imagine the wheeltray is a clock face, and rest your arms at what would be about twenty past eight. Place your hands on either side of the clay, thumbs pointing upwards. Now press inwards steadily and gradually until the clay rises upwards to form a cone. ◁

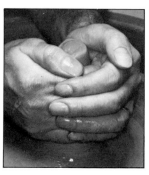

good idea to rest your forearms on the wheeltray whenever possible, as you will find that this gives you a more stable working position.

Successful throwing

There is no one correct way of throwing, as you will see if you watch other potters at work. Each has his or her individual mannerisms. You will find that your own style will emerge as you become more and more proficient. The throwing techniques illustrated here are the ones I have found to be most effective, but you should treat them purely as a starting point until you find, or develop, an individual and effective style.

You will need to lubricate both your hands and the clay frequently to prevent 'drag' (the clinging of the clay to your hands) during the throwing process. As soon as the clay begins to feel at all dry, or drags against your hands, pour a little water over it. If you are using a wooden wheelbat, slightly dampen it with a sponge before you begin to throw – this will help the clay stick

to it. If you are using a metal wheelhead, without a wheelbat, it should be left dry. If the surface is wet, the clay is likely to slip.

If you wish to take your hands away from the clay at any stage, relax gradually and decrease the pressure slowly. Throughout the entire process it is very important to carry out all actions as smoothly as possible, as any sharp or sudden movement will knock the clay off-centre. Also, never allow the clay to get out of control, or you will find yourself chasing uncentred clay round and round the wheel in endless circles.

Centring

The key to successful throwing is centring the clay correctly. Otherwise anything you produce will have weak, uneven walls or a poor shape. Practise the technique until you have perfected it. Wheelheads are usually marked with concentric circles for guidance. If you use wheelbats, you can mark concentric circles on them yourself with a pencil and compass.

3 Support your right hand with the left and cup it over the top of the clay. Then press downward with both hands to flatten the cone again. Repeat this two or three times. This process is known as coning and serves several purposes – it aids centring, forces any remaining air to the surface of the clay, and helps to condition the clay. When the clay begins to feel a little dry, pour a little more water over it. △

4 Place your forearms at a position of half-past seven. Put your right hand over the clay with fingers closed, their tips on the wheelhead. Support your right hand by gripping round it with your left. Make yourself as rigid as possible, locking all your muscles. Push downwards with your right hand, and simultaneously pull towards you with your left.

5 To check whether the clay is centred, touch the side lightly with the point of a tool or needle while it is rotating. If the clay is correctly centred, the point will mark the surface evenly around the whole of its circumference; if the clay is not centred accurately, the line will be broken or show signs of uneven pressure. As you gain in experience, you will develop a feel for centred clay, and find that such checks become unnecessary.

Throwing a shallow open form

Ideally, a shallow open form should have a heavy base and low thick walls. Practise the technique of opening the clay to make this basic shape until you have mastered it. As your confidence increases, try working with larger quantities of clay. You can use this form as a basis for making ashtrays, pet-food dishes, and in larger sizes for fruit or serving bowls.

1 Spread your centred clay into a flattened dome shape to a height of about 3-4cm (1⅛in or 1½in). The finished pot should eventually be no wider than the mass of clay now before you. Place your arms on the wheelhead as shown, supporting your right hand with your left. Reduce the wheel speed slightly. Press down on to the middle of the clay dome with the tip of your right thumb until a well has formed (see 1a). ▷

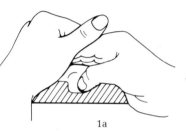

1a

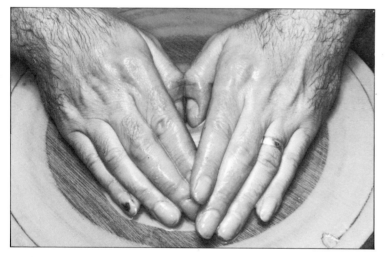

3 Gently pull both thumbs outwards (see 3a) to open the clay. Do not press downwards. Do not open the clay further than the width of the base, or the walls will collapse. △

2 Continue pressing your thumb into the centre of the clay until it is about 1.5cm (⅗in) from the wheelhead. Then remove your thumb and put a little water in the well. Place your hands on either side of the clay dome, and put both thumbs inside the well, wrapping your fingers around the clay (see 2a). △

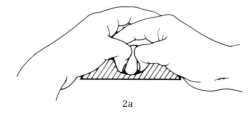

2a

3a

4 Using a sponge, carefully mop out all of the water from the inside base of the dish before stopping the wheel. △

5 Cut away any excess clay from the foot of the outside wall with a trimming tool, preferably leaving a slight undercut at the base – this will facilitate the dish's removal from the wheelhead. Hold the trimming tool lightly but firmly against the clay so that you do not remove too much clay at once. When you have finished trimming, allow the wheel to stop.

6 Hold one end of the cutting wire in each hand, and reduce its length until it can be passed just under the base of the clay without your hands snagging on the side of the pot. Keeping the wire taut, and as close as possible to the surface of the wheelhead, draw it carefully through the base of the pot. △

7 Flood the wheelhead with water, and pull the wire through once again in the same way, forcing water underneath the base. Wet a tile, or suitable board, and place it level with the wheelhead. You should now be able to draw your pot off the wheelhead and on to the tile or board by applying only a little pressure to the base of your pot. If the pot will not move easily, flood the wheelhead again and pass the wire through as before. ▷

Throwing a cylinder/1

When you have mastered throwing a simple shallow open form, the next step is learning to throw a cylinder. This shape provides the basis for many thrown shapes, including bottles, mugs and jugs.

As the wheel rotates, the centrifugal force of the wheel normally pushes the clay outwards. To make a cylinder, you must prevent this happening and make sure you draw your hands strictly vertically, never sideways, during the lifting process. You may find it helpful to stand, rather than sit, at the wheel while raising the walls of the cylinder. You can then lean right over the centre of the wheel quite easily. This helps you to line up the direction of the lift as you are actually looking down on the cylinder.

Take a 0.75kg (1½lb) ball of clay and centre it on the wheel. Shape the clay mass into a fairly short squat dome. Then, resting your forearms on the wheeltray at a clock position of twenty past eight, rotate the wheel at between half and three-quarters of its full speed.

1 Place your arms on the wheelhead as shown. Bring your right hand over the centre of the clay dome. Lower your right thumb steadily into the rotating clay until it is about 2cm (¾in) from the wheelhead.

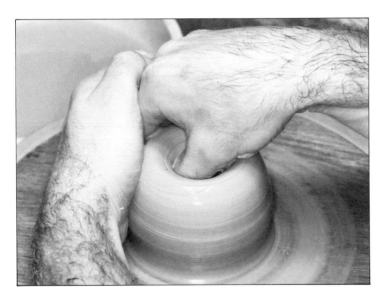

3 Holding the ridge between the tips of your thumb and middle finger, raise the clay with a smooth vertical movement of the hands (see 3a). Keep both arms on the wheeltray, and support your right hand with your left. △

2 Place a little water in the newly-formed opening and cup your right hand over the clay, with your fingertips just touching the wheelhead. Supporting your right hand with your left, move just the tip of your right thumb steadily outwards to open the clay. Then, keeping your thumb still, pull the fingertips of your right hand towards it (see 2a) – this gathers clay from the outside base to form a clearly visible ridge round the base of the clay.

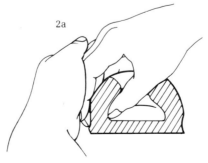

2a

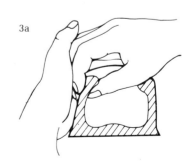

3a

4 The cylinder should now be about 8 or 9cm (3⅛ or 3½in) tall. If the walls remain thick, and you can still reach the inside base with your right thumb, repeat the gathering and lifting process. If you can no longer reach the inside base easily, you must change the position of your hand.

5a

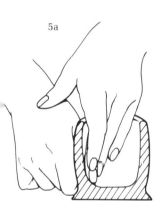

5 Hold your left hand straight. Tuck the other fingers behind the middle finger. Place your left hand inside the cylinder (see 5a) until you just touch the base. Clench the fingers of your right hand and turn the thumb outwards. Slide the tip of your right index finger about 1cm (⅖in) along the inside of your thumb. Place your right hand against the outside of the cylinder wall, pointing downwards. Make a bridge to your right hand with your left thumb. ▷

6/7 Rotate the wheel at half speed. Adjust your position slightly so that you are leaning right over the wheelhead. Tuck both elbows into your side. Gather a lifting ridge at the base between your right index finger and the tip of your left middle finger. Lubricate your hands well, and raise the clay ridge smoothly upwards between your left middle finger and right index finger until both hands are clear of the rim.

9 Allow the cylinder to rotate at least twice before you sever the rim completely and lift it away. Cut 0.5cm (¼in) below the lowest point of the rim. ▽

8 Repeat the lifting process if necessary. Then take a pin or needle firmly in your right hand. Place your right forearm on the wheeltray in a clock position of four. Place your left forearm on the wheeltray in a clock position of six. Steady the inside of the rim with your left index finger, slowly rotate the wheel and cut steadily and carefully through the clay wall. △

10 Gently mop out all the water from the inside of the cylinder, using a sponge attached to a stick. △

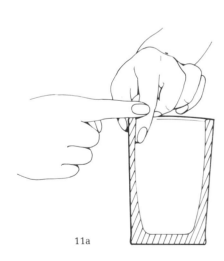

11a

11 To thicken and smooth the rim slightly, place your left thumb and index finger just below the top of the rim for support, and press gently downwards on the rim with the index finger of your right hand (see 11a).

12 Smooth the rim of the cylinder carefully using a damp sponge.

13 Cut an angle of 45° around the base of the cylinder using a trimming tool.

14 For quick removal, cut under the base of the cylinder with cutting wire as the wheel is still turning. Stop the wheel. Dry your hands and lift the cylinder firmly from its base, twisting and rocking it gently as you lift it from the wheel.

15 If you lack confidence, use the normal method of removal (see p77). You should use this in any case for delicate pots. ▷

Making a set of cylinders
Fix a stick to the side of the wheeltray at the appropriate angle and height for a guide. The tip of the stick should be set at rim level so that it just touches the side of the pot.

Swelling and collaring

The shallow open form and the cylinder provide the basis of most other thrown shapes. When you have mastered both these forms, you can apply the techniques of swelling and collaring to them to create an infinite variety of other forms. Make sure that the clay is well lubricated while you are throwing, but do not use too much water; if you do, the clay will eventually become too wet and your form will collapse.

Swelling

1 The tendency of the clay to move outwards means that very little pressure is required to swell a pot. To make a swelled form, first make a short, squat cylinder.

2 To swell a clay form from the base, crook the index finger of your right hand on the outside of the clay wall, so that it is slightly higher than the middle finger of your left hand on the inside of the clay (see 2a), as you begin the lifting process. ▷

2a

3 To swell from above the base, apply pressure from the inside with the fingertips of your left hand. Work upwards, supporting the clay from the outside with your right hand. Form a bridge between both hands with your thumbs (see 3a). ◁

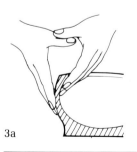

3a

4a

4 Smooth and thicken the rim slightly, by pressing it gently with your left index finger. Support the inside rim with the middle finger of your left hand, and the outside with your right hand as shown (see 4a).

Collaring

1 This technique is used for narrowing or constricting the shape of a clay form, and can be used for making a bottle, as shown here. First, throw a cylinder in the normal way, but make the wall slightly thicker than usual. This can be trimmed when the form is leatherhard, if necessary *(see pp88-9).*

2 Point the tips of your thumbs upwards and close your hands around the clay. Coax, rather than force the clay to narrow by applying gradual pressure with your thumbs and index fingers.

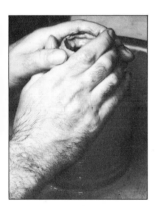

3 As the clay is compressed it also thickens. This means that you have enough clay to repeat the lifting process, and raise a new section of clay if you wish.

4 Insert your left middle finger into the collared rim and draw the clay upwards. Support the rim from the outside with your right index finger.

5 Draw the neck of the bottle to the required height. Once shaping is complete, trim the rim and smooth it with a sponge. ▷

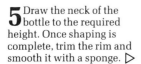

Swelling and collaring/2

You can collar a thrown form until it closes completely to form an egg-shape or sphere. Enclosed thrown forms can be cut open to make pots or jars with integral lids *(see p97)* or they can simply be used for ornamental purposes.

These forms also provide excellent bases for modelling or sculpture *(see p16)*. Alternatively, they can be painted *(p142)*, pierced *(p135)* or incised *(see p132)* to marvellous effect.

Closing

1 Throw a gently swelling form with a thick base and rim. Sponge out any excess water from the inside base and collar the clay.

2 Continue to exert a gentle, gradual inward pressure until the hole at the top closes completely. ◁

Inflating a full-bellied pot

The shape of full-bellied or spherical forms can be improved by inflating them gently after they have been thrown. This gives the shape of such pots a subtle fullness. To inflate a pot, cut a small hole in a piece of paper and lay it over the neck of the pot. Place your mouth over the hole and blow slowly and gently until the walls of the pot swell very slightly to create a rounded effect.

Once you have mastered the shaping techniques, you can produce a wide range of work – experiment with different bottles, jars, cache pots, plates and bowls.

Making a plate

Plates and dishes can be functional, purely decorative, or both. In either case, they provide ideal pieces of work for testing different types of decoration or glazes. For example, try experimenting with the various types of slip decoration (see pp140-3) and using the dish as the framework for a pictorial design painted with colouring oxides (see pp136-7).

To produce a plate approximately 30cm (11⅘in) in diameter you will need a ball of clay weighing about 4kg (8.8lb). If you do not throw the plate on a wheelbat, you should leave it to stiffen slightly on the wheelhead before you attempt to remove it. It is always advisable to do this with wide or large forms, which can easily be distorted or damaged if they are removed from the wheel when the clay is still soft.

1 Throw a shallow open form with a thick base and sides. Flatten the rim with your left hand, supporting the clay from beneath with your right hand. Do not make the rim completely horizontal; give it a slight upward tilt to prevent it flopping or collapsing. ▷

2 Smooth the rim further with a rubber kidney, still supporting the rim from beneath with your right hand. △

3 Trim the rim, if necessary, by pushing a needle or pin slowly and gradually through the clay, taking care not to tear the rim. Smooth the plate with a sponge.

Making a bowl

Bowls are amongst the most popular pottery forms. Apart from being both practical and useful as containers, they also provide marvellous shapes and surfaces on which you can experiment with various decorative techniques. Although there is one basic bowl form, every slight variation on this can create a completely different effect. Try making a range of bowls, concentrating on producing subtle differences in shape and form.

Bowls are made by gently swelling the walls of a basic shallow open form. They can be thrown individually, but sets of smaller bowls can also be thrown one after the other from a single piece of clay during one working session using a technique known as stack throwing.

Making a bowl

1 Open the clay, making sure you leave quite a thick wall. Raise the wall, supporting your right hand with your left (see 1a). ◁

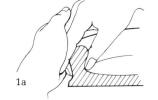

1a

2 Maintaining a steady pressure, thin and swell the clay, drawing the wall upwards and slightly outwards with your right hand (see 2a).

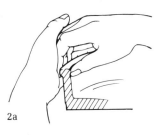

2a

3 Crook your right index finger and place it against the outside surface of the clay wall. Position the fingertips of your left hand on the inside of the clay wall just below your right index finger. Form a stabilizing bridge as shown between both hands with your left thumb.

4 Draw your hands upwards, continuing to swell and raise the wall *(see 4a).* Maintain the stabilizing bridge between your hands – you will find this gives you better control over the shaping of the bowl. ▷

4a

5a

5 Support the rim from beneath with your left hand and, using the tip of your right index finger, press gently on the rim to shape it *(see 5a).*

6 Trim the excess clay from the base of the bowl. Try to avoid pressing too hard, as you may push the bowl off centre.

7 A footring gives an elegant shape. It can be turned when the bowl is leatherhard *(see pp88-9).* ▽

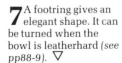

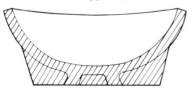

Throwing several small bowls
Form a tapered cone from centred clay and throw a bowl from the top section of the cone. Cut through the clay beneath the base of the bowl with twisted cutting wire while the wheel is still turning.

Remove the bowl, stand it on the shelf of the wheel and continue to throw the next one.

Trimming

The removal of excess clay from the outside and underside of the base of any thrown form is called trimming or turning. It should not be used as a means of altering or correcting a badly-thrown shape and should be kept to a minimum.

Pots should be trimmed when they are leatherhard; at this stage the clay should pare away in long thin shavings. If the clay is too dry, it will come away as fine powder; if it is too wet, it will not come away cleanly and small pieces of clay will be left sticking to the surface of the pot.

2 To ensure the base is level, draw a turning tool across it from the centre – if the tool marks the clay evenly, the base is level. Define the outline of the footring on the sides and base of the pot with a pointed tool.

Carefully shave away the clay from outside the line of the footring on the sides, using whichever trimming tool you find most comfortable and effective. ◁

Trimming

1 Recentre the pot, base upwards, on the wheelhead. Check that the pot is centred and attach it gently but firmly to the wheelhead with a few small pieces of plastic clay. Supporting the base of the pot and your right hand with your left as shown, trim away ragged edges with a needle.

3 Working from the centre outwards, shave the clay away from the base to hollow out the area inside the footring. Steady the end of the tool with your left index finger.

4a

4 To complete the footring, make an undercut of 45° around the edge of its outside line. This not only provides a neat finish (see 4a) but also makes it comfortable to hold if you glaze it using either the dipping or pouring method of application (see pp118-9).

Trimming awkwardly-shaped work
If a pot is too unstable to be trimmed normally, it can be supported in a chuck, which is centred and fixed to the wheelhead during trimming. Chucks can be leatherhard clay collars made individually for specific pieces, or can be improvized from different-shaped plant pots. Here various types of pots are shown (1, 2, 3, 4 and 5), each with their appropriate chuck (1a, 2a, 3a, 4a and 5a).

Trimming with a chuck
Place a coil of clay round the rim of the chuck as a cushion and insert the form to be trimmed. Trim as usual.

Trimming a lid
The ideal chuck for a lid is the actual pot for which it was made. Secure it to the rim of the pot with pieces of clay.

Trimming wide dishes
For wide dishes with thin rims, use a chuck that allows the form to rest comfortably over, rather than inside, it.

Throwing large forms

Throwing large amounts of clay on a wheel requires quite a lot of physical strength. If you find this difficult, you can still produce large pieces of thrown work by joining two or more thrown sections together. These are known as composite pots. Making such pots requires particular care, if you are to avoid bulges or splits at the joints, and bad proportions. Before you begin, make a sketch of your intended form and divide it into sections that can easily be thrown separately.

Throwing a large jar

1 Throw a deep, but not very wide, bowl on a wheelbat with a thick, flat rim. Throw a second bowl of the same size *(see p148)*, but with a base at least 5cm

(2½in) thick. Leave both bowls to stiffen. Place the first bowl on the wheelhead. Score both rims and coat them with slurry. Raise the second bowl by its wheelbat, and invert it on the first.

2 Check that the inverted bowl is centred correctly before fixing it firmly in place. Remove the wheelbat from the inverted bowl with a cutting wire. Cut a hole in the clay at the top of your joined form, just large enough to take your hand. ◁

Composite pots

Throw the base section, and measure its proportions carefully with calipers *(see pp148-9)*. Remove the base and throw the next section. Leave both the sections to dry until they are leatherhard.

Recentre the base section on the wheel and score the rims of both sections. Check that the upper section is correctly centred and join the two sections firmly together with stiff slurry.

3 Start the wheel and throw a neck or rim for your jar, from the thick layer of clay, in the same way as you would normally.

Throwing coiled additions

1 A third alternative when producing large thrown forms is first to throw as large a form as possible on the wheel. Allow this to stiffen slightly, and then add a thick coil to the rim of the form. Make sure this is flush with the rim.

2 Fix the coil in place with slurry and then secure it by stroking the clay downwards into the outside rim with your thumb. ◁

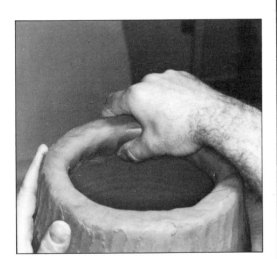

3 Smooth the clay downwards into the inside rim with your thumb. This ensures that the coil is securely fixed before you begin throwing.

4 Start the wheel and lift the coil. An uneven rim will probably develop. Trim this away before you add the next coil. Continue to add and lift the clay coils in this way until your form has reached the desired shape and size. ▷

Altering thrown shapes

The round, symmetrical shape of a thrown pot can be altered in various ways after throwing is completed to make a variety of shapes. However, you cannot disguise a badly-thrown or badly-centred pot by altering its shape, as the fault will still be apparent afterwards. If a pot is badly thrown it is best to discard it and start again.

Making a cylinder oval

1 Throw a cylinder. With a taut cutting wire, cut about 1cm (⅖in) into the clay wall just above the base on opposite sides of the cylinder. ◁

3 When the pot is the required shape, trim away the excess clay from the base. Then smooth the clay from the base upwards into the wall with a plastic kidney to seal the outside join. Seal the inside join with a sponge or by applying a little slurry with a stick. ◁

2 Exert gradual pressure on opposite sides of the pot just above the lines of the cut until the pot becomes oval.

Beating

A thrown pot can be given a number of flat sides by beating it when it is leatherhard with a flat piece of wood. Support the pot with one hand as you beat it.

Flattening a thrown cylinder

Throw a baseless cylinder and press it between both hands to form a flattened oval. Roll a slab of clay (see p60) until it is almost the same thickness as the walls of the cylinder. Place the cylinder on the slab and mark around the base with a pointed tool.

Remove the cylinder and cut out the base. Attach it to the bottom of the cylinder with a little slurry and smooth the join with a sponge.

Making an oval vase

1 Throw a tall cylinder which narrows and then flares gently outwards at the neck. Invert the pot, and mark an oval section across the diameter of the base. Carefully cut out this section.

2 Using a ruler, mark a vertical line from each end of the oval section on the base to the rim of the pot with a pointed tool. Score along the line.

3 Score around the inside of the oval section, apply a little slurry and press gradually and gently on both sides of the pot until it closes completely.

Altering the shape of a neck

The necks of thrown forms can be altered quite easily by pressing gently on opposite sides of the neck of the pot with the palms of both hands until it becomes elliptical in shape (right). The body of the pot should remain round. The shape of the neck can be accentuated by pulling the narrow ends of the rim gently outwards with both index fingers (below).

4 As the base is closed, the sides of the pot will split down the score lines. To fill these, apply slurry down the splits and smooth a thin coil in place.

Making and fitting lids/1

A lid should be seen as an integral part of a pot and should be thrown during the same session as the body. It is vital that lids are precisely measured to ensure that they fit properly. This can be done quite easily by first measuring the diameter of a pot's rim with calipers, and then accurately throwing a lid to the same dimensions (see pp148-9).

When the actual pot is made, a seating for the lid must be made at the rim. This may be in the form of either an inside or outside gallery, unless a pot is thrown with an integral lid (see p97).

Making a pot with an inside gallery

1 Throw a thick-rimmed cylinder. Flatten the rim by pressing it gently with the side of your right index finger, while supporting it with your left hand. Check that the rim is level and trim it if necessary.

2 Support the outside rim with your right index finger and the inside rim with the fingertips of your left hand. Position your left thumb tip over the inner half of the rim and push it vertically into the clay. ◁

3 Press steadily downwards with your left thumb until the inside gallery begins to form. Support both the inside and outside of the rim with the fingers of your right hand to prevent it becoming distorted.

4 Smooth and square the gallery with a right-angled tool or a small rectangular piece of wood. Use your left hand both to support the rim of the pot and steady your right hand.

5 Trim the rim if necessary and then smooth both the gallery and the rim with a sponge. Take great care not to distort the gallery, as this will make fitting a lid difficult.

Making a pot with an outside gallery

1 Collar the neck of a thick-rimmed cylinder. Trim the rim. Press on the outer half of the rim with your right index finger. Support your right hand and the inside rim with your left hand. ▷

Making a cup lid

A simple cup-shaped lid to rest on an external gallery can be made from a small upturned thrown bowl. ▽

2 Take a right-angled tool, or wood rectangle, in your right hand. Smooth and square the gallery.

3 Trim the clay below the gallery and then smooth it with a sponge to define the line of the lid seating more clearly.

Making a casserole

To make the body of the casserole, throw a form with a rounded body that narrows slightly towards the rim. Form an internal gallery in the rim. Measure the diameter of the casserole from inside rim to inside rim.

Throw a shallow open form and flatten out the rim to form a flat dish shape. Open the clay until the diameter is the same as that of the inside rim of the casserole body. When it is approximately the right width, trim it with a pin or needle to the exact size. To check that the lid fits snugly when you have trimmed it, place it on two thick, long strips of paper and lower it gently into

the rim of the pot. The lid can be left to dry resting on the actual gallery. When the casserole and lid are leatherhard, some type of lug or handle should be attached (see pp98-101).

Making and fitting lids/2

Making a lid for an internal gallery

1 Press the tips of both index fingers into the clay, about 1cm (⅖in) from its centre. Open the clay, allowing a small pillar to form in the centre.

2 Open the clay further to the required width with your left hand, supporting the outside base with the middle finger of your right hand to prevent it spreading.

3 Keeping your right hand in the same position, open the clay over your right middle finger with your left hand until the upper rim of the lid is the appropriate width.

4 Check the width of the base and upper rim of the lid to ensure that it will sit snugly on the gallery (see pp148-9). Open the lid further, if it is too small.

5 Trim the lid with a pin or needle, so that it will fit precisely in place. ▷

6 To form the knob, apply pressure at the base of the central pillar with the fingers of both hands.

7 The knob can be hollowed if you wish by pressing the tip of your left index finger into its centre. ▷

8 This type of lid can be fitted directly into the throat of a pot, as well as on to an internal gallery. ▽

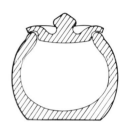

Making a flanged lid

This can be used for a pot with a level rim, as the flange will keep the lid in place. Throw a thick-rimmed shallow open form or bowl to the appropriate width. Support the rim with your left hand and depress the outer edge of the rim with your right thumb as you would to form an external gallery. Square and smooth the flange with a right-angled tool or small wood rectangle. A knob can be added to the lid once it has become leatherhard and has been trimmed.

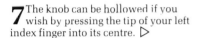

Making a pot with an integral lid

Pots with integral lids can be made from enclosed thrown forms (see p74). Leave a small piece of extra clay at the point where you close the form and shape this into a knob. Allow the form to stiffen slightly.

Using a pin or needle, carefully cut a wavy line around the whole circumference of the pot about a third of the way down the body. This wavy cut will provide a stable join between the lid and the body.

Remove the lid from the body and trim both cut edges with a sharp knife. Sponge them smooth.

Making handles

Handles should be considered as decorative as well as functional. When you have mastered the basic techniques of making handles, experiment with your own ideas. Thrown pots are best complemented by what are known as 'pulled' handles – lengths of clay that are drawn out by hand.

Drying and attaching handles

Pulled handles should be left to stiffen slightly before they are attached to a pot. Ideally, at the time of application, they should be firm enough to maintain their shape and to be easily handled without fear of distortion, but soft enough to be pliable. To stiffen a pulled handle, fix it to a table so that it hangs over the edge and the air can circulate around it – this will allow it to dry evenly. Pulled handles should not be attached to pots that have dried beyond the leatherhard stage. If the pot is too dry, the join between the pot and handle will crack open. A handle rarely needs to be left for longer than an hour to stiffen, and you should check it at regular intervals to make sure it has not dried out too much.

You will find that handles always dry more quickly than the pots to which they are attached. In extreme cases this makes them prone to crack. To prevent this happening, wrap polythene round the handle during drying, where possible, and allow the pots to dry very slowly during the initial drying stages. Handles are very fragile at the greenware stage. Never pick up a pot that has not been biscuit fired by its handle.

If the handle is attached to a pot while it is still too soft, it may begin to sag. If this happens, turn the pot upside down to correct the problem.

Alternative handles

The simplest handles can be made by dragging a piece of wire, bent to form a rectangular loop at one end, through a block of prepared clay. The shape and size of the handle can be altered simply by using a different-sized loop.

To make the wire loop, take a piece of wire, fold it in half, and begin to twist the open ends together. Leave the loop of wire untwisted to the size you require and form it into a rectangular shape.

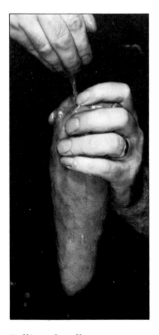

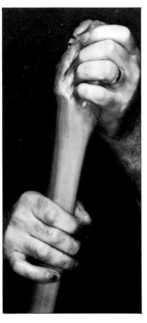

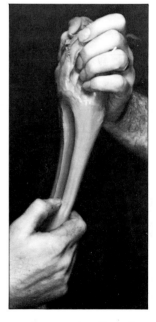

Pulling a handle
1 Pat a 1-kg (2.2-lb) ball of clay into a carrot shape. Grip the thick end in your left hand, and hold it at about eye level. Trickle some water down its length.

2 Wet your right hand. Form the thumb and index finger into an 'O' shape and stroke firmly down the full length of the clay. Apply pressure evenly on every side of the handle.

3 As the handle lengthens, form a 'U' with your right thumb and index finger. Turn your right hand through 180° at each alternate stroke so that the shape of the handle develops evenly.

4 When your handle is of the right width and length, make a groove down the centre with your right thumb. Attach the handle to a table so that it hangs over the edge. Leave it to stiffen.

A pulled handle can be attached to the top of a lid. This is particularly suitable for casserole lids. To do this, allow the handle to stiffen as usual and then cut it to the required length. Smooth each end into the surface of the clay, so that it becomes an integral part of the lid.

Making several handles
To make handles for a set of pots or mugs, pull one long handle and then cut off sections of the appropriate length. Form each section into an arch and leave them to stiffen on a board. △

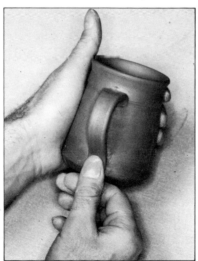

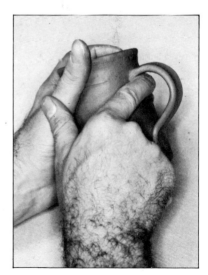

Fixing the handle
1 Score the points to which the handle will be attached. Cut your handle to the required length, cutting through the clay at an angle of about 45°.

2 Attach the top of the handle with thick slurry, supporting the inside of the pot with your left hand. Check that the handle can keep its shape, and fix the bottom end in position.

3 Make sure that the handle is strictly vertical. Smooth the joins at the top and bottom of the handle with your index finger or thumb, and then finish them off with a damp sponge.

Making a jug

Traditional jugs have gently-swelling bodies that narrow at the neck and flare open at the rim. However, even if you stick to this classic shape as a basis for making your own jug, the size and the proportional relationships of each of the elements can be varied. It is well worthwhile experimenting with the different possibilities to see how wide a variety of forms you can produce.

Making a jug

1 Shape a cylinder to create the basic jug form. Leave a thicker rim than usual, so that the spout can be formed without difficulty.

2 Form your left thumb and index finger into a downward-pointing 'V' shape and rest them on the outer rim at the point where the lip is to be formed. ◁

3 Lubricate your right index finger well with water. Place it between the 'V' of your two left fingers and move it back and forth from left to right, pressing gently so the lip gradually begins to protrude outwards. To stop the movement affecting the rest of the rim, restrict it with your left finger and thumb.

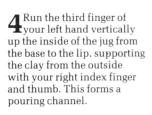

4 Run the third finger of your left hand vertically up the inside of the jug from the base to the lip, supporting the clay from the outside with your right index finger and thumb. This forms a pouring channel.

5 Accentuate the line of the channel by scoring gently down its outlines with your thumb. Leave the pot to dry until it is leatherhard, when the handle can be attached. △

Experimenting with traditional jugs
You can use the basic techniques shown here to make jugs of many different shapes and sizes. Each should have its own individual character, but whatever style of jug you choose to make, remember that it must be comfortable to hold, easy to pour and a convenient size for its purpose. ◁

Pulling a jug handle
1 Score the point below the rim opposite the lip. Attach a clay carrot firmly in place with stiff slurry.

2 Hold the pot horizontally in your left hand so that the handle hangs down vertically. Pour a little water over it and lubricate your right hand.

3 Having attached the top of the handle, pull it in the usual way (see pp98-9) until it is of the required thickness for the jug.

4 Score and apply slurry to where the bottom end of the handle will be joined. Fix this in place and then break off any excess clay. △

5 Make a final check to ensure that the handle is not crooked. Smooth the joins at the top and bottom of the handle into the surface of the jug with a damp sponge. Accentuate the handle joins if you wish by using your thumbs to draw them in a curve into the body.

Making lugs and knobs

Lugs are solid handles that are used where strength and support are vital, as in the case of a casserole dish. They can also be used in conjunction with ordinary handles to give extra handholds on heavy jugs or jars.

There are several different types of lugs. When you choose a design, remember that they should complement the body of the pot. Where two lugs are attached to opposite sides of a pot, you must check that they are both equidistant and level. Before attaching them, look at the pot from above and then from the side to make sure they are positioned correctly.

Throwing a knob on a lid
1 Centre the lid on the wheelhead and fix it firmly but gently with a few pieces of plastic clay. Score the centre where the knob is to be formed and apply some thick slurry.△

2 Position a small ball of prepared clay on the lid and press it firmly in place. Smooth it roughly into shape.

3 Start the wheel and shape the knob, applying more pressure around the base to create a mushroom shape.

Attaching pulled lugs

Lugs can be cut from an ordinary pulled handle. Position them carefully on the pot as usual. Score the appropriate points on the pot and fix the lugs in place with a little slurry. Trim them with a knife and blend them into the surface of the pot with a sponge, as you would for thrown half-cylinder lugs.

4 Finish the knob by smoothing with a damp sponge. Smooth the join between the knob and lid.

Attaching large thrown lugs

1 Measure the circumference of the pot with a length of string. Having done this, fold the string in half and hold it against the pot again to give you two halfway points at which to fix the lugs. △

2 Throw a shallow cylinder without a base. Allow it to stiffen slightly, and then cut it carefully in half with a sharp knife. Score and apply slurry to the points on the surface of the pot to which the lugs will be attached. ◁

Attaching thrown lugs

Small thrown cylinders can be used for lugs or knobs, which can be attached to the sides or lids of pots. When you have thrown the number of lugs you require, score and apply slurry to the appropriate point on your pot. Position the lugs and press them gently but firmly into place, taking care not to distort or damage them.

3 Fix the lugs in place, taking care not to damage them. Trim them to the size you wish, making sure that this is proportionate to the pot. For the best effect, tilt the lugs upwards and cut the sides at a slightly downward angle. ◁

4 Blend the lugs into the sides of the pot, smoothing all the joins carefully so that they become invisible. Smooth the outer edges of the lugs.

Making a teapot

To create the body of the pot, make a short, stumpy cylinder from 1.36kg (3lb) of clay. Raise and thin the wall, keeping the top 1-2cm (²⁄₅-⁴⁄₅in) thick. Collar the rim until the opening is no more than 6-8cm (2²⁄₅-3¹⁄₈in) wide. Gently swell the body of the pot and trim the rim, if necessary. Press on the rim with your right index finger to flatten it and create an inside gallery *(see pp94-7)*. Trim the base and sponge away any excess water from inside.

Remove the body of the teapot from the wheelhead. Keep it nearby for reference while you are making the spout, the handle and the lid.

Making the spout
1 Make a baseless cylinder from 340g (³⁄₄lb) of clay. Raise the wall and collar it after each lift to narrow it.

2 Use only your left index finger inside the cylinder as you raise the clay. As you taper the spout further, use your little finger instead.

3 Make the spout as thin as possible. Flare the rim slightly outwards. Leave the pot, spout and lid until they are soft-leatherhard.

Making the lid

Take the rim measurements of the pot to give you the proportions of the lid *(see pp148-9)*. Form the clay into a flattened dome. Open it to the appropriate width. Position the tip of your right thumb 1.5cm (³⁄₅in) from the centre of the clay. Lower it to within 1cm (²⁄₅in) of the wheelhead to create the knob. Hollow this with your right index finger.

Place your right index finger on the wheelhead, just touching the outer edge of the clay. Open the clay over this finger with your left index finger to the appropriate width.

4 Shape the base of the spout so that it fits snugly against the pot at an angle of about 45°. The lip should be no lower than the gallery.

6 Attach the spout to the pot with stiff slurry. Make sure that its base fits the pot's surface. Trim the tip, cutting it a little to the left – a thrown spout twists slightly in a clockwise direction during firing. ◁

5 Trim the body and lid, ensuring that the lid fits snugly. Pierce a hole in the lid and bend the flange slightly outwards at one point to hold it in place during pouring. Pull a handle (see pp98-9) and allow it to stiffen while you fit the spout in position.

When you have established the spout's position, mark lightly round its base with a pointed tool. Remove the spout and pierce as many straining holes as possible within the marked area. Hold the piercing tool at about 45°. △

7 When the spout is soft-leatherhard, gently form the end into an effective pouring channel.

8 Attach the handle (see pp98-9). Make sure that it is vertical and in a straight line opposite the spout.

Teapots with character
Teapots can be made in a variety of styles. By altering the position of the handle, the shape of the spout or lid, you can create teapots of many individual characters.

Firing, glazing and decorating

If you ask any potter which part of his work is the most exciting, the answer is likely to be opening the kiln door when the final firing has been completed to see the fired work within. Until this moment, you can never be quite sure what the glazes, colours and textures you have used will look like. No two firings will ever produce identical results and the slightest variations in firing temperature can affect colour, texture and glaze. For this reason, it is important to control the kiln temperature carefully and to keep careful records of your firing schedules for reference. Although I have given comprehensive instructions for firing electric kilns, taking some of the possible influences into account, every kiln is slightly different. You will learn by experience how best to control your own firings. It is inevitable that some of these will not be completely successful but *Fault finding* on *pp150-5* will help you to analyse and correct any mistakes.

Glazes can be bought from pottery suppliers, or can be prepared from a mixture of raw ingredients. Recipes for a variety of glazes have been given here, but you should also try experimenting with combinations of different ingredients to produce your own glazes – remember that it is often a personal glaze that adds the perfect finishing touch to an individual piece of ceramic work.

Clay can be decorated at almost every stage of the pottery process and all of the most important techniques are given here. You can control the clay's texture and colour; you can cut, impress, pierce or model its surface; and you can colour it with glazes. These are just a few of the possible choices. However, before you use any decorative technique, colourant or glaze, it is worth experimenting first on a piece of work that is not particularly important.

Firing/1

The kiln

An electric kiln is the best all-round choice, as it is easy
to operate and maintain. There are two basic types –
front-loading and top-loading. Although front-loading
kilns are the easiest to load and unload, top-loading
types are cheaper and more compact, and so are usually
preferred by amateurs.

Electric kilns are fitted with heat controls and safety
devices to ensure safe and effective firing. It is also
worth installing a door interlocking or isolation switch,
if such a device is not a standard fitting, to ensure that
the kiln door cannot be opened while the kiln is on.

Basic kiln maintenance

Once a kiln is installed *(see pp46-7)*, it requires little
maintenance. However, it is important to have the
wiring checked by a qualified electrician every two or
three years, or more often if the kiln is in frequent use.

It is inevitable, after a time, that the kiln will begin to
show signs of wear and tear, and cracks may appear in
the interior brickwork. These can be filled with
proprietary refractory cement, which is available from
kiln suppliers. Brush a little water into the cracks before
filling them, as this will help the cement adhere more
readily. It is not possible to eliminate all the cracks,
however, since the cement shrinks when it is fired and
new finer cracks appear. Fine cracks are not a problem.

Cleaning the inside

Even over a short period of time, considerable amounts
of debris will collect in the grooves housing the
elements, particularly around the floor. All but the
largest pieces of debris can be easily removed with a
domestic vacuum cleaner. When you do this, take care
not to disturb the elements as they become very fragile
after a few firings.

The kiln's outer casing

The vapour produced during firing eventually stains,
rusts and corrodes the kiln's metal casing, particularly
around the doors, lids, spyholes and bungs. The
strongest vapours are emitted during the early stages of
biscuit firing, so it is always advisable to leave spyholes
and bungs open until a temperature of 600°C is reached.
This allows the vapours to escape freely from the
chamber, thereby reducing the amount of corrosion to
the kiln.

Any obvious signs of rust should be cleaned away at
once, using a stiff wire brush. Once cleaned, the
framework can be painted with a special heat- and rust-
resistant paint if so required.

Kiln shelves

These are expensive to replace and so should be looked

Stacking the kiln shelves
Each shelf should be
supported at three points as
shown here.

after carefully. When they are not in use, they should be
stacked on end, rather than horizontally on top of one
another. If possible, make a rack to provide upright
storage space.

A shelf will last longer if it is not fired to the
maximum temperature it can tolerate, so if possible use
shelves that can withstand temperatures higher than
those to which you usually fire.

To protect the shelves, they should be coated with a
substance known as batwash, which can be bought or
made up from a mixture of 80 per cent alumina, 20 per
cent china clay and water. A good coat of batwash will
protect the shelves from glaze runs which can then
usually be removed with minimal damage to the shelf.
A fairly thick coating of batwash should be used on the
shelf to provide good protection.

As an alternative, dry alumina can simply be
sprinkled across the shelf surface to provide what is
known as placing sand. This has the advantage of
allowing the clay to shrink freely during firing, while
eliminating the danger of splitting. Also, placing sand
can simply be brushed off after firing. This means that
any shelves can be turned over for the next firing to
correct any slight warping if necessary. The one
drawback is that placing sand can fall, or easily be
brushed on to work on the lower shelves.

When you load the kiln for firing, support the
shelves at three points – one support at each of the two
corners on one side, and one support in the centre of the

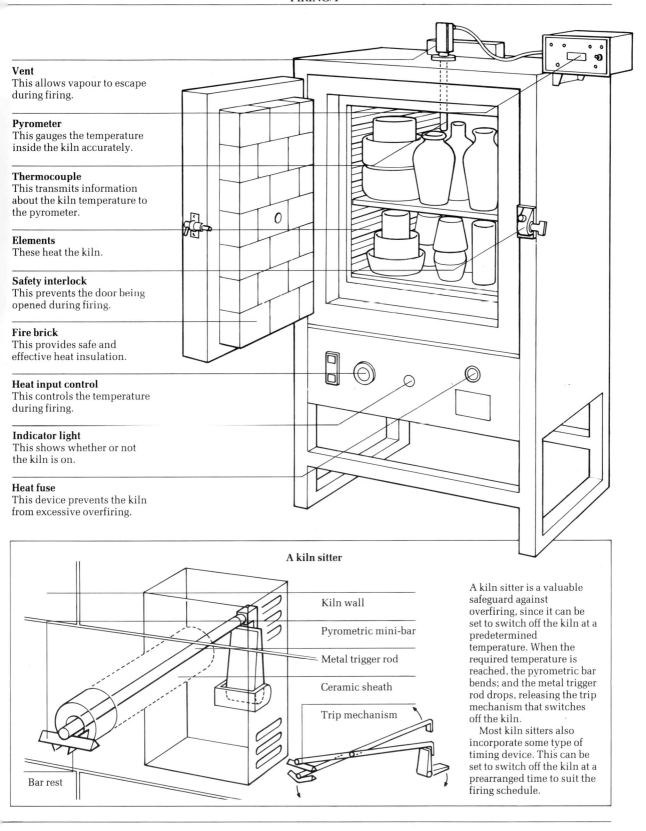

Vent
This allows vapour to escape during firing.

Pyrometer
This gauges the temperature inside the kiln accurately.

Thermocouple
This transmits information about the kiln temperature to the pyrometer.

Elements
These heat the kiln.

Safety interlock
This prevents the door being opened during firing.

Fire brick
This provides safe and effective heat insulation.

Heat input control
This controls the temperature during firing.

Indicator light
This shows whether or not the kiln is on.

Heat fuse
This device prevents the kiln from excessive overfiring.

A kiln sitter

Kiln wall

Pyrometric mini-bar

Metal trigger rod

Ceramic sheath

Trip mechanism

Bar rest

A kiln sitter is a valuable safeguard against overfiring, since it can be set to switch off the kiln at a predetermined temperature. When the required temperature is reached, the pyrometric bar bends; and the metal trigger rod drops, releasing the trip mechanism that switches off the kiln.

Most kiln sitters also incorporate some type of timing device. This can be set to switch off the kiln at a prearranged time to suit the firing schedule.

Firing/2

opposite side. This makes the shelf stable, and also spreads the load efficiently. The props for each shelving tier should be placed directly above each other.

The elements

The elements actually heat the kiln. They are made from spiral wire with straight tail ends that connect them to the electrical circuit. They are fitted into housing grooves on the sides and floor of the kiln.

Kiln elements are made of 'Kanthal wire' and are available in two grades: Kanthal A and Kanthal A1. Kanthal A elements allow firings of up to 1200°C, Kanthal A1 elements allow up to 1300°C. With careful use, a set of new elements should last several years, although this depends on how often the kiln is used. To make the elements last longer, fire the empty kiln before you use it. This allows each element to develop a protective oxidized layer, which gives it greater durability. Elements will last longer if the kiln is not fired to its maximum recommended limit. For example, if the maximum recommended temperature is 1300°C, ideally you should not fire to beyond 1280°C.

Packing the kiln

Ensure that your shelves are perfectly flat, as clay fired on warped shelves is liable to warp itself. The tiers of shelving should be staggered to allow the heat to be distributed evenly throughout the kiln. For the same reason, there should be a gap of at least 4-5cm (1⅗-2in) between shelves and elements.

Always pack the kiln as economically and as stably as possible. First divide the items you wish to fire into roughly similar heights. The shortest items should be packed on shelves at the bottom of the kiln – this ensures the most stable kiln load. However, if you have awkwardly-shaped or heavy objects, these may have to go at the bottom of the kiln.

Packing for biscuit firing

As your work is not glazed at this stage, it does not matter if one item touches the next. Similarly-shaped items can be stacked rim to rim, or footring to footring, as long as the pieces at the foot of the pile can take the weight. This form of stacking is known as boxing. If necessary, to save space, one piece of work can be placed inside another.

Although clay shrinks overall during firing, it expands slightly during the initial heating process, so you should not wedge the pots too tightly, and you should leave a small gap at the sides and the top of the kiln chamber.

In every kiln there are variations in temperature, and there will be spots which are hotter or colder than anywhere else. These should not affect biscuit firing.

Kiln furniture
Refractory bats or shelves (1) are available in various sizes. They can be supported by tubular props (2) or interlocking props (3), which can be fitted one on top of the other. Prop collars (4) can also be bought to give the props extra support. Stilts (5) are used to fire pots which are completely coated with glaze, to prevent them sticking to the shelves. ▷

Packing for a glaze firing

It is important that glazed pieces do not touch each other during firing, as they will stick together. A minimum space of 0.5cm (⅕in) should be allowed between each item. More shelves will be necessary as only one layer of items per shelf is possible.

The bases of stoneware glazed pots must be wiped clean of glaze. However, earthenware glazed pots should be completely glazed to ensure that they are non-porous. In order to prevent them sticking to the surface of the shelf, stand them on proprietary stilts. To make loading easier, position the shelf props before putting the glazed pieces on the shelf. Take great care not to damage the glazed surfaces of the pots when you load the shelves.

Operating the kiln

The input of heat into a kiln is controlled by a regulator, which is either marked in terms of low, medium or high settings, or in percentages. The kiln must be at the right temperature at the right stage to ensure successful firing. The temperature is indicated by the colour inside the chamber but a more accurate indication of the correct heat can be given by placing pyrometric cones – ceramic cones that will soften and bend at a specific temperature – inside the kiln.

A complete range of pyrometric cones is available, each of which bends at a different temperature. This temperature and an identification number are marked on the side of each cone. For accurate firing, you will require three cones – one that melts at the firing temperature you require; one that melts at a slightly lower temperature to indicate that the kiln is nearing the required temperature; and one that melts at a slightly higher temperature to indicate the danger of overfiring. The cones should be set in soft clay or proprietary holders and placed in the kiln prior to firing in line with the spyhole, where they are easily visible. When the appropriate temperature is reached, the cone will bend over.

Pyrometric bars, which work on the same principle, are also available. If you use these, the kiln can automatically be switched off once it has reached the required temperature, if necessary, by using a kiln sitter. This device is frequently used on top-loading kilns to cut off the power supply to the kiln at the appropriate moment.

A continuous and accurate indication of the temperature inside the kiln can be obtained through the use of a thermocouple and a pyrometer. A thermocouple consists of a pair of long, thin metal strips, protected by a porcelain sheath, which is

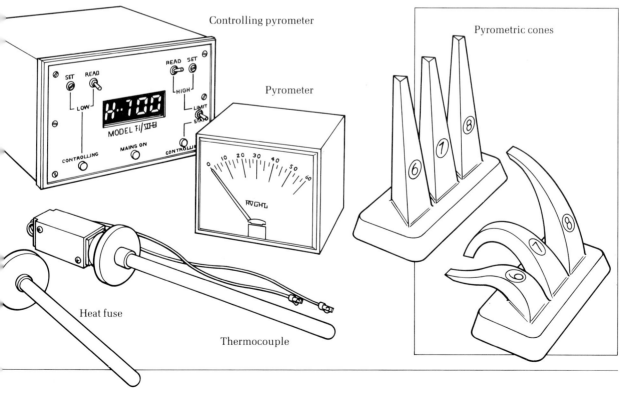

Controlling pyrometer

Pyrometer

Pyrometric cones

Heat fuse

Thermocouple

Firing/3

inserted into the kiln. As the temperature begins to rise, the thermocouple produces a small electrical charge, which shows as a temperature reading on the pyrometer – this can conveniently be mounted on a wall near the kiln. Before firing, it should be set to room temperature, not 0°C.

A wide range of temperature-controlling systems of various levels of sophistication are available. Complicated or expensive systems are not necessary, but it is worth buying a system which will cut off the power at a set temperature, as well as maintaining a set temperature for a fixed length of time or indefinitely.

Drying for biscuit firing
It is vital that your work is dried properly before it is biscuit fired. Even in a warm environment, this may take over a week; if the room is cold it will take considerably longer. To test whether clay is dry, check its colour – this should have become lighter – and also that it no longer feels cold to the touch – the cold is a sign of dampness. Remember that the base of any piece

of work always takes the longest time to dry, since the air cannot circulate around it and it is often the thickest part of the pot. If possible, turn the pot upside down once the rim or top has dried to allow the base to dry more quickly and thoroughly.

Pre-heating for biscuit firing
To help the clay dry thoroughly before firing, you should load the kiln with the work to be fired and pre-heat it the day before the biscuit firing. This is particularly valuable with thick work, work of varying thicknesses and once-fired ware.

Load the kiln, and set the kiln's simmerstat to 10 per cent – or set the equivalent heat input regulator at low – for an hour or so until it reaches about 100°C. Switch the kiln off, replace the bungs and close the spyhole. Leave your work in the kiln until the following day to give the clay the chance to dry out thoroughly.

Biscuit firing
Work is normally biscuit fired to between 950°C and

The kiln – interior colour and corresponding temperatures	
No visible colour until approx 500°C	
First signs of very dark red	500-550°C
Dark to deep red	550-700°C
Deep to cherry red	700-800°C
Bright cherry red	800-900°C
Red/orange	900-1050°C
Bright orange	1050-1100°C
Pale orange to yellow	1100-1200°C
Yellow to yellow white	1200-1280°C

Approximate bending temperature of orton cones			
Cone	Temperature rise in °C per hour		
	60°C	100°C	150°C
08	945	950	955
07	973	978	984
06	991	995	999
05	1031	1036	1046
04	1050	1055	1060
03	1086	1092	1101
02	1101	1110	1120
01	1117	1127	1137
1	1136	1145	1154
2	1142	1150	1162
3	1152	1160	1168
4	1168	1176	1186
5	1177	1186	1196
6	1201	1210	1222
7	1215	1227	1240
8	1236	1248	1263
9	1260	1270	1280
10	1285	1294	1305
11	1294	1304	1315

Packing for a glaze firing
These two pictures show a kiln which has been correctly packed for a glaze firing both before (*left*) and after (*right*) firing. The pottery has been stacked as economically as possible and the weight of the load has been distributed evenly. None of the pots are touching each other.

Pyrometric cones (*set on the second shelf down*) were used to indicate the temperature. Note how all three cones have melted in the second picture, indicating a slight overfiring.◁

Biscuit firing schedule, with and without carbon soak
The graph shows the rate of temperature rise in hours for an average biscuit firing. You can record your own firings for reference.

1 Take out the bungs.
2 Turn the heat input regulator to low (simmerstat 5-10 per cent).
3 Leave the kiln for 4-6 hours or until the temperature reaches 200°C.
4 Turn the heat input regulator to medium (simmerstat 45-50 per cent).
5 Leave the kiln for another 4 hours or until the temperature reaches 600°C.
6 Put in the bungs.
7 Turn the heat input regulator to high (simmerstat 100 per cent).
8 If a carbon soak is required from approximately 800-850°C to dispose of any carbon materials in the clay (*see Fault finding*), turn the regulator to medium (simmerstat 80 per cent) for an hour and then to high (simmerstat 100 per cent).
9 When the temperature reaches 950-1000°C, turn the kiln off and leave it to cool. Do not open the door before the temperature has fallen below 200°C.

Switch off kiln at 950-1000°C.

Turn kiln to full after carbon soak if necessary.

Carbon soak period – kiln turned down slightly.

Bungs put in at 600°C – kiln turned on to full.

Kiln setting turned up from low to medium at 200°C.

DEGREES CENTIGRADE

1200

800

400

100

HOURS

1

4

8

12

16

Firing/4

1000°C, but you cannot immediately turn the heat input regulator to high. The temperature rise must be carefully controlled throughout.

Adapting the schedule
Timings of firing depend on the thickness of work you are firing, how open the clay is, and how densely the kiln is packed. New kiln elements also tend to perform more efficiently than old ones, which often take longer to reach the required firing temperatures. For example, if the kiln load consists only of thin, thrown ware, made of well-grogged clay, the firing schedule may be slightly faster than usual. At the other extreme, if the load to be fired consists of thick work, or a mixture of sculptured and thrown objects, it is wise to follow a slightly slower firing schedule.

Keeping a firing log
Every kiln is slightly different, so it is important to become familiar with the rate at which the temperature increases in your kiln. Make notes on the timing,

settings, and temperatures of all your firings. Also note whether the bungs are in or out, or the spyholes open or closed. All these factors can be plotted on a graph. Keeping a firing log of this kind will help you to understand your kiln, and firing in general.

Glaze firing
Individual glazes require different firing temperatures *(see pp116-7)* and you should test-fire any new glaze on a small tile before using it on your work. Experiment until you have found the correct firing temperature.

Underfiring and overfiring glazes
You should look carefully for any signs of underfiring and overfiring in your experiments. Underfired glazes will look dry and dull, while normally shiny glazes will look matt or cloudy. Most underfired glazes can be fired again to the correct temperature, without altering the end result.

Overfiring, however, cannot be corrected – you will simply have to start again from scratch. Slight

Overnight firing
The following graphs show schedules that are suitable for overnight biscuit and glaze firings.

Biscuit firing
1 Open the bungs.
2 At 12 noon, set the heat input regulator to low (simmerstat 10 per cent).
3 At 4pm, the temperature should have reached about 200°C. Turn the heat input regulator to medium (simmerstat 45 per cent).
4 At about 8.30am, the temperature should be 600-800°C. Provided that it has reached at least 600°C, turn the heat input regulator to high (simmerstat 100 per cent) and put in the bungs.
5 At about 10.30am, when the kiln reaches a temperature of 950-1000°C, switch it off and leave it to cool.

Stoneware glaze firing
1 Open the bungs.
2 At 4pm set heat input regulator to medium or to 85 per cent.
3 At about 8.30am, the temperature will have reached approximately 1000°C. If so, close the bungs

and turn the heat input regulator to full (100 per cent) until the glaze maturation temperature is reached.
4 At about 10.30am, the firing should be complete. Switch off the kiln. Do not open the door before the temperature falls to below 200°C.

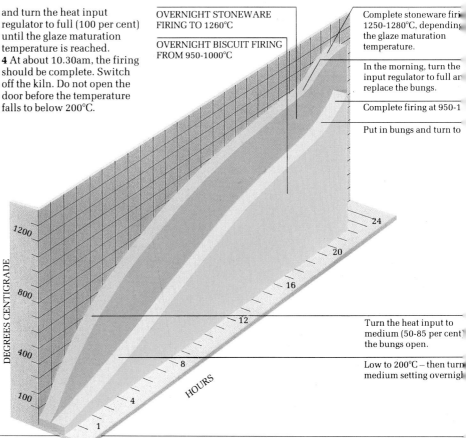

OVERNIGHT STONEWARE FIRING TO 1260°C

OVERNIGHT BISCUIT FIRING FROM 950-1000°C

Complete stoneware firi 1250-1280°C, depending the glaze maturation temperature.

In the morning, turn the input regulator to full an replace the bungs.

Complete firing at 950-1

Put in bungs and turn to

Turn the heat input to medium (50-85 per cent) the bungs open.

Low to 200°C – then turn medium setting overnigh

DEGREES CENTIGRADE

1200

800

400

100

HOURS

1

4

8

12

16

20

24

Firing thick pieces of work
Fire large and solid pots or sculptures slowly to prevent them breaking. (This sculpture was made by Nicholas Marangos, student.)

overfiring may cause impurities in the clay to bleed through the glaze, but if pottery is drastically overfired, the glaze will become more fluid and may run on to the shelf; the clay may 'bloat' (see Fault finding) and/or vitrify; and matt glazes will become shiny and blistered. In very extreme – and rare – cases, the kiln furniture may collapse.

Once-fired ware
Most pottery is biscuit, and then glaze fired, but greenware clay can be glazed and then fired only once. However, this does have disadvantages. The water content of the glaze may break down the clay structure, causing the pot to collapse (see pp118-9). Also, glazing mistakes cannot be corrected and more flaws are produced than usual. For once-firing, the kiln should be packed as for a glaze firing.

The firing schedule should be as for a normal biscuit firing until at least 600°C. After this, the kiln can be turned up to full until it reaches the appropriate earthenware or stoneware temperature.

Glaze firing schedule
The graph shows three examples of suitable glaze firing schedules (for stoneware, earthenware and once-fired stoneware). All of them show a slow approach to the glaze maturation temperature and include a period of soaking (that is, maintaining the glaze at its maturation point for about one hour).
1 Take out the bungs.
2 Turn the heat input regulator to medium (simmerstat 50 per cent). Leave the kiln for an hour to allow the water in the glaze to evaporate before putting in the bungs.
3 Turn the heat input regulator to high (simmerstat 100 per cent). However, if the glaze you are using requires a slower firing, turn it to medium (simmerstat 50 per cent) to allow a slow heat build-up. Then turn it to high (simmerstat 100 per cent).
4 When the maturation temperature of the glaze is reached (see pp116-7), turn off the kiln and allow it to cool down.

5 If a glaze soak is required, maintain the maturation temperature for an hour before turning off the kiln.
6 When the temperature drops below 200°C, open the kiln door and carefully unload your work.

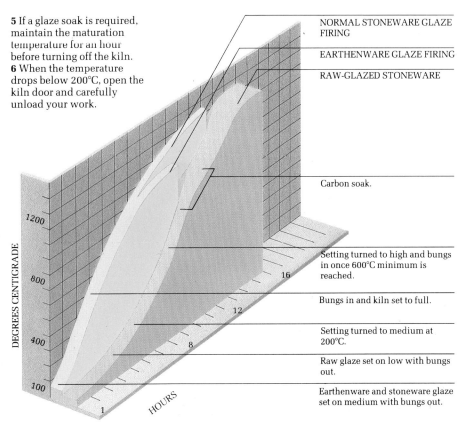

NORMAL STONEWARE GLAZE FIRING

EARTHENWARE GLAZE FIRING

RAW-GLAZED STONEWARE

Carbon soak.

Setting turned to high and bungs in once 600°C minimum is reached.

Bungs in and kiln set to full.

Setting turned to medium at 200°C.

Raw glaze set on low with bungs out.

Earthenware and stoneware glaze set on medium with bungs out.

DEGREES CENTIGRADE

1200

800

400

100

HOURS

1

8

12

16

Glazing/1

Glaze is just as important in creative ceramics as forming and firing. Although basic prepared glazes can be bought in powdered form, these are satisfactory only for beginners as, although they are very reliable, the choice available is limited. Once you have gained in experience, you should try making glazes to suit your specific needs, and experimenting with various glaze recipes *(see pp124-5)*.

A simple prepared transparent or clear glaze, bought from a supplier, is the most straightforward and reliable glaze for a beginner. Provided that it is fired to the recommended temperature, it will make any pottery suitable for holding food or drink. Colouring oxides can also be added to simple transparent glazes to make different-coloured glazes.

Preparing a bought transparent glaze

Buy at least 10kg (22lb) of glaze at a time – this will produce two bucketfuls of prepared glaze. The glaze is supplied in the form of a white powder. Any colouring oxides are added to this powder in the required percentage *(see pp146-7)*, and then the dry ingredients are mixed with water.

To make one bucketful of glaze, weigh out about 5kg (11lb) of glaze powder. Measure out the appropriate amount of colourant if necessary. Take two large plastic buckets. Place the dry ingredients in one, and pour in about 0.5l (17½fl oz) of water per 1kg (2.2lb) of glaze powder. Leave the mixture for a few minutes so that the glaze can absorb the water – this prevents any glaze dust from floating into the air as you stir the mixture. Mix the glaze by hand, breaking up any large lumps of powder between your fingers. Add more water if necessary until the mixture has the consistency of thick, lumpy cream.

Shovel
Use this, rather than your bare hands, for dealing with raw materials.

Measuring jug
This should be used for measuring the required amount of water.

Sieve
A 60 mesh sieve should be used for sieving bought glazes; finer sieves – up to sizes of 120 mesh – are necessary for making a glaze from a recipe.

Lawn brush
This is used to pass the glaze mixture through the sieve.

Wooden rails
These provide a convenient support for the sieve while the glaze mixture is passing through it.

Preparing a bought glaze
1 Weigh the required amount of powdered glaze.

2 Measure out the required amount of water and add it to the glaze powder. Stir the mixture thoroughly.

3 When the glaze is the consistency of thick, lumpy cream, pass it through the sieve into the other bucket.

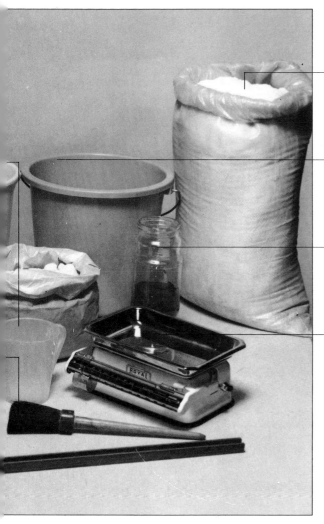

Glaze ingredients
Prepared glazes and
individual ingredients are
supplied in powder form.

Buckets
You need one for mixing
glaze with water, and one
into which to sieve the
prepared glaze mixture.

Jars
These are useful for storing
colouring oxides.

Scales
These should be capable of
weighing up to 5kg (11lb).

Place two wooden rails across the second plastic
container and rest a 60 mesh sieve on them. Transfer
the glaze mixture into a jug, and then pour the mixture
into the sieve. Push the glaze through the mesh with a
lawn brush. If the glaze mixture is too thick to pass
through the sieve easily, add a little more water to thin
it further.

When all the glaze has been sieved, stir it well and
check its consistency – this should now be the same as
single cream. If the mixture is too thin, leave it to stand
until the glaze particles and water have separated; then
pour off some of the excess water and stir the glaze until
it acquires an even consistency again.

Before you use the glaze, stir it again thoroughly. If
you leave it for more than a few days, some of the water
in the mixture will evaporate and you will need to add
more and stir the mixture again. If too much water

evaporates, the glaze will collect as a hard sticky mess
at the bottom of the container. If this happens, you will
need to add more water and sieve the glaze again before
you use it.

Glazing for earthenware firing
At earthenware temperatures, clay remains quite
porous. As a result, if you are firing pottery intended to
hold food and drink at these temperatures, it must be
glazed completely inside and out. As the base of the pot
will also need to be glazed, it must be fired on a
three-pointed stilt to prevent the glaze on the base
sticking to the kiln shelf. After firing, the stilt should be
knocked away from the pot base. You will find that
small splinters will remain embedded in the base of the
pot. These should be removed with a carborundum
stone – never try to pick the splinters off with your
fingers as they will be razor sharp.

Glazing for a stoneware firing
Clay fired to stoneware temperatures will become
non-porous, whether or not it is glazed. If the pot is to
be glazed, you should leave the base uncoated when
applying the glaze – otherwise it will stick to the shelf
of the kiln. Before firing, you should also clean off any
glaze from the sides with a sponge to approximately
2mm (1/25in) from the base of the footring to allow for
the glaze running slightly.

Glazing/2

Applying the glaze

Glaze is usually applied to clay at the biscuit ware stage, when the clay is still quite porous, but no longer fragile. There are three basic methods of applying glaze – dipping, pouring and spraying. The method you use depends on the size and shape of pot you are glazing and the way in which it has been decorated.

Dipping

The quickest, and simplest, way to glaze a small pot is to immerse it totally in a bucket of glaze. Make sure that you have sufficient glaze, and then take the pot by its rim and base between your thumb, index and middle fingers. Holding the pot at an angle, slowly and steadily lower it into the glaze, base first, so that the inside fills with glaze. Twist the pot gently to make sure that the whole surface is covered. Hold it in the glaze for only 2-3 seconds – otherwise the coating may be too thick. This in turn will increase the risk of the glaze running when the pot is fired.

Invert the pot, remove it from the glaze, and gently shake any droplets from the rim. Do not touch the glazed surface until it is dry – it only takes a minute or so for the porous clay to absorb the glaze's water content. After this you can handle the pot, although you must be careful not to chip or mark the glaze.

Touch up any bare patches or fingermarks by adding blobs of glaze with a brush or your finger until you have created a slightly thicker layer of glaze than elsewhere. When the patch is dry, gently rub it with your finger until it merges into the rest of the glaze.

Glazing the inside and outside of a pot separately

Pour one glaze into the pot. Swill it round until the

Dipping
1 Lower the pot, base first, into the glaze.

2 Make sure the inside fills with glaze. Remove the pot, twisting it as you do so.

3 Touch up any fingermarks or bare patches with a brush or your fingertip.

4 Wipe the glaze away from the base and the sides just above the base.

1 Glazing a teapot
Pour glaze inside the teapot.

2 Swill the glaze around until the inside is completely covered.

3 Cover the spout and immerse the pot in the glaze to coat the outside.

Pouring
Pour the glaze over the pot, working from the base in one smooth swift movement as you rotate it. Work on a whirler if possible.

Poured patterns
A pattern of arches can be made by pouring the glaze from the base in straight lines. Hold the jug slightly away from the pot's surface.

Hold the lip of the jug against the surface of the pot as you pour glaze from the base. The stream of glaze produces a V-shaped pattern down the side of the pot.

surface is covered completely and pour out the remainder. When the glaze has dried, remove any glaze that has run on to the outside surface by scraping it first with a knife and then wiping it off with a damp sponge.

Provided that you have enough glaze and the pot is small enough to fit into a bucket, you can glaze the outside with a different glaze by immersing it. Hold the pot at the base, and lower it vertically, rim first, into the glaze. Provided that you lower the pot absolutely vertically, the pressure of the air inside the pot will prevent the glaze entering the pot and only the outside will be glazed.

Pouring

You can glaze the inside of a pot, which is too large to be easily immersed in glaze, by pouring glaze inside it and then swilling it around until the whole of the inside surface is covered. The outside surface of the pot is then coated by pouring glaze over it. To do this, hold the pot upside down at the base over a plastic container.

Fill a jug with glaze and pour the glaze over the pot, working from the base in a smooth and swift movement, so that the outside surface is completely covered before any of the glaze has a chance to dry.

If you are glazing a bowl, hold it upside down like an umbrella, balancing it on your hand from the inside. If it is particularly large or heavy, place two rails across the top of the container and rest the inverted pot on them. If you have a whirler, place the plastic container on it, so that you can slowly rotate the pot as you pour the glaze. If the pot has been resting on rails, touch up the bare patches where the pot has been in contact with them, using a brush or your finger.

Poured or dipped patterns

You can produce glaze patterns by altering the way you dip or pour your glaze. A pot can be dipped first into two different glazes in succession to create an even double coating, for instance – this is known as double dipping. Alternatively, the pot can be dipped into one glaze and then dipped into another at a different angle to produce uneven layers of glaze – this technique is known as window dipping.

You can also produce distinctive patterns by altering the basic pouring technique slightly. Experiment by holding the pot at different angles when you apply the glaze. This will alter the way the glaze runs over the surface. Try holding the jug close to the pot surface and then a few centimetres away from it.

Raw glazing

With this technique, the clay is glazed while it is at its greenware stage and then fired once, this one firing incorporating the effects of both the biscuit firing and glaze firing. Greenware clay is particularly fragile, which makes applying the glaze more difficult than usual. Never lift a greenware pot by a handle or its rim – always hold it at the base.

Pouring and spraying (see pp120-1) are the best techniques to use for applying glaze to once-fired ware. Because greenware clay will still absorb water, you must be careful not to apply too much glaze – otherwise the clay will become saturated and the pot may collapse. To prevent the risk of this happening, it is advisable to glaze the inside of the pot first, and then glaze the outside approximately 24 hours afterwards when the inside surface is dry.

Glazing/3

This technique is particularly useful for applying glazes to irregular clay forms, sculptural pieces and extra-large pieces. However, the equipment necessary for spraying is expensive and so often comes low in a home potter's priorities. For spraying glaze safely and successfully, you need a spray gun, a compressor, a spray booth with a fitted extractor fan and filter, an approved face mask and a whirler.

Put on the mask before you begin work. Pass the prepared glaze through a 120 mesh sieve – this minimizes the risk of the spray gun becoming blocked. Place the piece of work you intend to glaze inside the spray booth on a whirler and switch on the compressor and extractor fan. Fill the gun with glaze and holding the gun at least 45.7cm (18in) away from the pot you are spraying, gradually build up the layers of glaze. You should take special care to ensure that you spray all the awkward areas – around handles, lugs and rims, for example – thoroughly. To check that the clay is properly coated with glaze, use the point of a pin to scratch through a tiny patch on the glaze.

The subtle effects that can be produced by spraying glaze means that the technique is perfect for a variety of decorative techniques. Colouring oxides can also be sprayed in the same way as glaze. Try graduating or fading one glaze into another with the spray gun and using a wax resist. Spraying glaze over underglaze decoration will also prevent the design from smudging.

A simple spray kit
If you only need to glaze a piece of work by spraying occasionally, you can buy a fairly simple and inexpensive spray kit. This consists of a spray head, a spray jar and a disposable air compressor. ▷

Spraying equipment
The piece of work to be glazed is placed inside the booth so that the excess spray can be contained. The extractor fitted to the booth removes glaze particles from the air. △

Using resists
1 Having applied one layer of glaze, place the paper resist on the clay surface.

2 Apply the second glaze carefully with the spray gun until the exposed clay surface is thoroughly covered. Then peel away the resist

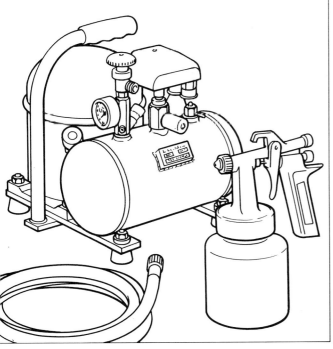

Spray gun and compressor
Air from the compressor forces the glaze from the gun in a fine spray. The gun must only be used with the booth (*above left*) and face mask.

Glazing awkwardly-shaped work

Spraying was the ideal way of glazing the piece of work shown here (made by Suzie Gray), which was too large and too complex to be glazed by dipping or pouring. Using a spray meant that glaze could be applied evenly all over, and that every hollow and fold could be easily covered.

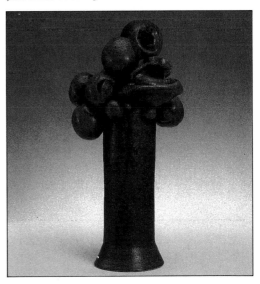

Glazing/4

Understanding glaze

The three basic elements of glaze are silica, alumina and a flux. Silica is the substance that gives the glaze its essential glass-like quality. Its normal melting point is over 1700°C, which is about 400°C above the maximum temperature at which most kilns operate. A flux, which lowers the melting point of silica, therefore needs to be added to the glaze mixture. Alumina is a stabilizer, and is the ingredient that makes the glaze form an effective coating on the clay surface.

A number of raw materials contain silica, alumina and a type of flux in varying amounts. Few of these substances are suitable for use by themselves for making glazes and so need to be mixed together. The combination of different ingredients in glazes also affects the firing temperatures they require. The temperature at which a glaze vitrifies to form its characteristic glassy coating during firing is known as its maturation point.

Frits

Lead, borax and sodium are the commonest fluxes used at earthenware temperatures. In their ordinary state, none of these is suitable for use – lead is highly poisonous, borax dissolves too readily and sodium reacts violently to water. However, each of these is available in a 'fritted' form, which is both safe and easy to use. In a frit, the basic substance is combined with silica to form a glassy material, and ground to a powder. At earthenware temperatures of between 1000°C and 1100°C, frits need only a small amount of alumina as a stabilizer to be suitable for glazes by themselves, as they already contain silica and a flux.

Glaze ingredients

All the substances described here are common glaze ingredients. Each has its own particular qualities, but to find out how each responds in different mixtures under different firing conditions you must experiment yourself (see pp126-7).

Alkaline frit

This is a combination of sodium, potassium and silica – all fluxes – in an insoluble form. Most alkaline glazes are prone to crazing (see Fault finding) but borax can be added to the glaze to counteract this. Alkaline frits are used for crackle glazes, which use the crazing pattern as a decorative feature.

Alumina

This acts directly as a stabilizer and increases a glaze's viscosity. It can also be mixed with water to be used as a batwash for kiln shelves or left dry to be used as placing sand (see pp108-11).

Ball clay

This is a common working clay and contains both alumina and silica.

Barium carbonate

This is used as a secondary flux at stoneware temperatures and produces matt or semi-matt surfaces at earthenware temperatures.

Bentonite

This is a suspending agent – that is, it helps to suspend the particles of glaze powder solution – when added in quantities of up to three per cent.

Borax

This is a powerful flux at earthenware temperatures, and is generally used in its fritted form. Borax is a good alternative for lead, when a leadless glaze is required. It often produces slightly milky glazes which can be combined with oxides to produce interesting colours. However, iron oxide is a less effective colourant in borax glazes than in lead glazes. Small amounts of borax can also be added to stoneware glazes to lower their melting point.

China clay

This contains alumina and silica. It is particularly useful for colourless glazes, as it is relatively free of iron, which is a strong colourant. It can also be used to make a shiny glaze matt. Because it is very refractory, it can also be used to raise a glaze's maturation point.

Colemanite (calcium borate or borocalcite)

This is a powerful flux at earthenware temperatures. It can also be used as a flux in stoneware glazes, although its effects are not as strong. It intensifies the colours produced by colouring oxides.

Dolomite (calcium magnesium carbonate)

This is a source of calcium and magnesium, both of which strengthen the effects of colouring oxides. Dolomite is also a secondary flux – that is, it is not an effective flux by itself, but can be used in conjunction with another flux. It produces matt opaque glaze surfaces at stoneware temperatures.

Feldspars

Feldspar comes in a variety of different forms, but always contains silica, alumina, and fluxes, namely soda, potash and lime. It is an essential ingredient of all stoneware glazes, but forms a poor glaze when used by itself. The variation of the percentages in which soda, potash and the fluxes are combined makes some forms of feldspars preferable to others, depending on the firing temperatures used. They are used in earthenware glazes as secondary fluxes.

Feldspar-potash (orthoclase) should be used when a recipe simply states 'feldspar'. It contains more potash than soda. Feldspar-soda (albite) contains more soda than potash, and its melting temperature is lower than potash feldspar.

Nepheline syenite is a form of feldspar that contains more soda and potash than silica, and has a relatively low melting point compared to other feldspars. It is therefore used as a substitute for other feldspars where a lower maturation point is required.

Cornish stone (china stone or pegmatite) is a type of feldspar which has a higher silica content than usual. This causes it to melt at a slightly higher temperature than other feldspars.

Ilmenite
This is generally used in quantities of about two per cent with rutile to produce textured glazes. It is also useful as a colouring pigment for stoneware glazes.

Lead
This is used in its fritted form of lead bisilicate or lead sesquilicate. It is a powerful and popular earthenware flux, due to its ability to produce a reliable, smooth and relatively flawless, shiny glaze. Lead glazes produce rich colours when used with colouring oxides.

Fritted leads bought from manufacturers have a low lead solubility and, provided that they are used in strict accordance with the manufacturer's recommendations, can be used safely for pottery destined for domestic use. However, you should not use copper colourants in lead glazes on pottery intended for food and drink, as it increases the amount of lead released from the glaze.

Magnesium carbonate
This is a high temperature flux. When it is used in quantities of up to ten per cent it produces a buttery or satin matt glaze surface. If used in greater amounts, pinholing (see Fault finding) tends to occur.

Rutile
This is a mineral, which, when used in quantities of three to eight per cent by itself, or with ilmenite, produces mottled colourings.

Silica (flint and quartz)
Silica is the essential glass-forming ingredient in all glazes. It is found naturally in all clays and woodash, although it is also available in the forms of flint and quartz. These are both used to introduce pure silica into glazes. They also help to raise the melting point and to inhibit crazing.

Talc (magnesium silicate – French chalk)
This contains a high percentage of magnesium, which affects the colour and texture of a glaze, and silica. It also helps to increase the viscosity of a glaze. It can be used to produce a creamy satin or waxy glaze surface.

Whiting (limestone, chalk, calcium carbonate)
This adds calcium to glazes, which strengthens the effects of colourants. It is used as a flux when introduced in small quantities. When used in quantities of over 25 per cent, it makes the glaze matt.

Zinc oxide
This is used as a secondary flux in quantities of up to five per cent. When used in quantities of over ten per cent it produces a characteristic frosty, matt surface. If too great a quantity is used it can lead to glaze flaws, such as pinholing and crawling (see Fault finding).

Woodash
The fine white or grey ashes produced by wood fires can be used a basis for subtle, soft stoneware glazes, as they contain silica, alumina and alkaline fluxes as well as a small percentage of metal oxides. The proportions in which these ingredients are present vary with different types of woodash.

You will also find that two batches of woodash, even from the same type of wood will produce a slightly different glaze. Some types of woodash will melt to form a glaze by themselves in temperatures over 1250°C. When combined with up to 50 per cent of local clay, woodash often produces particularly interesting variegated yellow and rust red mottling. Although woodash can be bought, it is expensive and it is quite easy to prepare your own.

Preparing your own woodash
Collect about a sackful of the fine light-coloured ashes from any wood-burning fire. Try to avoid the blackened semi-burnt charcoal. Pour the ash into a large container and cover it with water. Stir the mixture with a stick – do not use your hands as the mixture is quite caustic – to bring any unburnt charcoal to the surface. Skim off the charcoal.

Sieve the mixture through a very coarse sieve – an ordinary garden sieve is ideal – to remove any large particles. Repeat the process with a 60 or 80 mesh sieve. You can sieve the mixture again through a 100 mesh sieve if you want a finer texture.

Allow the mixture to settle, and then pour off the water at the top. Add fresh water, stir the mixture again, and then allow it to settle. Repeat this washing process once a day for the next two or three days. Then leave the ash to dry to a powder. It is now ready for use.

Glazing/5

Glaze recipes can be obtained from various pottery magazines and books, and often from professional potters who are prepared to pass on their personal secrets. When following a recipe, tick off each ingredient as you add it to the mixture. Many of the raw materials used for glazes look very similar and it is easy to forget which ingredients you have or have not added. Any colouring oxides should be added to the mixture at the dry stage. When the ingredients have been weighed,

place them in a plastic container, add water and mix them as usual (see pp116-7). Sieve the mixture using a 100 or 120 mesh sieve.

Glaze recipes
It is vital to experiment with new and different glazes. A variety of recipes are given here but your results will probably not be exactly as stated here, because different batches of ingredients, firing conditions, thicknesses of

Glaze recipes
The following glazes are for stoneware temperatures and mature at Cone 8 (1240-1260°C). The quantities for each recipe are given in terms of proportionate parts per volume.

Transparent
Feldspar potash 40
Flint 30
Whiting 20
China clay 10

Gloss white glaze
Feldspar potash 40
Flint 30
Whiting 20
China clay 10
Zirconium oxide 12

Shiny green glaze
Feldspar potash 40
Flint 30
Whiting 20
China clay 10
Copper oxide 2.5

Shiny blue glaze
Feldspar potash 40
Flint 30
Whiting 20
China clay 10
Cobalt 1

Slops glaze
This attractive glaze is made from glaze leftovers.

Matt white dolomite glaze
Feldspar potash 48
China clay 24
Dolomite 25
Whiting 3

Note – this produces a smooth matt glaze, which can be combined effectively with colouring oxides.

Green dolomite matt
Feldspar potash 48
China clay 24
Dolomite 25
Whiting 3
Copper oxide 2

Dark oatmeal glaze
Feldspar potash 50
China clay 30
Dolomite 28
Whiting 6
Red iron oxide 5

Stone-textured glaze
Feldspar potash 53
Whiting 36
China clay 11

Note – this produces a frosty surface which responds well to colouring oxides.

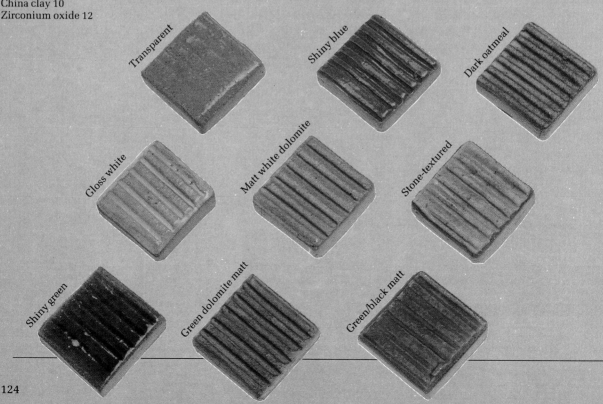

application and types of clay influence the final result.

Not all glazes are suitable for use on once-fired ware (see pp112-15). However, the recipes given below for brown-black glaze, mottled rust ash glaze and green dolomite matt glaze are particularly good.

Testing a glaze batch
You cannot take it for granted that any given glaze recipe will perform exactly as expected. It is therefore advisable to mix up a small amount first to fire as a test before using it on any of your work. No more than a total dry weight of 100g (4oz) is needed for a glaze test.

Test your glaze on a sloping surface, as this shows the flow of the glaze. If you draw a line around the edge of the glazed area with iron oxide before you fire it, you will be able to detect any glaze flow. It is essential that you keep a careful record of any glaze tests you make, giving a complete description of the results of each.

Green/black matt glaze
Feldspar potash 53
Whiting 36
China clay 11
Copper oxide 3

Note – this produces a green matt glaze with black streaks and dark specks.

Dry ash glaze
Woodash (mixed) 50
China clay 50

Note – this produces a very dry surface, and a good base for colouring oxides. It provides a very pleasing finish to sculptural work.

Mottled rust ash glaze
Woodash (mixed) 50
Red earthenware clay 50

Traditional woodash glaze
Feldspar potash 40
Woodash 40
China clay 20

Bright honey glaze
Feldspar potash 33
Flint 32
Whiting 20
China clay 15
Zinc 15
Red iron oxide 5

Shiny to matt rust brown glaze
Flint 35
Whiting 25
Feldspar potash 13
China clay 13
Red iron oxide 16

Tenmoku brown glaze
Cornish stone 55
Whiting 12
Flint 18
China clay 6
Bentonite 2
Red iron oxide 10

Note – this produces a pleasing dark brown glaze, which breaks to a rust colour.

Mirror black glaze
Cornish stone 88
Whiting 12
Bentonite 2
Red iron oxide 12

Brown/black glaze
Red earthenware clay 55
Borax frit 41
Red iron oxide 4

Raw glazes
The recipes for brown/black glaze, mottled rust ash glaze and green dolomite matt are suitable for raw glazes.

Dry ash

Bright honey

Brown/black

Mottled rust ash

Shiny to matt rust brown

Mirror black

Traditional woodash

Tenmoku brown

Slops glaze

Glazing/6

Making opaque glazes

These are made by adding an opacifier to a base glaze. You should experiment with the various opacifiers available by themselves and in conjunction with colouring oxides (*see pp136-7*).

Tin oxide is the most effective opacifier. It produces a characteristic blue-white. It can be used at all temperatures and approximately 10 per cent will produce full white glazes. However, it is expensive. Zirconium oxide is a cheaper alternative, although it produces harsher whites. Ten to fifteen per cent is required for strong whites. Titanium dioxide produces creamy white glaze in quantities of up to 10 per cent.

Experimenting with glaze ingredients

Divide a slab of clay into small sections and biscuit fire it. Mix about half a teaspoon of several raw glaze materials with a little water to form a thin paste. Apply a different material to each section of the slab with a brush and then paint the appropriate name underneath with iron oxide.

Fire the slab to a temperature of 1000°C. You will find that only the frits melt at this temperature. Refire the slab to 1250°C, and see what happens. Some materials will have melted completely, some will have partially melted, and others will have become dry and flaky. This simple test will show you which materials are almost glazes by themselves and suitable components for glazes.

Repeat the above experiment, this time using mixtures of two different raw materials. Try the following combinations first.

Glaze tests

The raw materials shown here have each been fired first at 1000°C (shown on the light-coloured clay) and then at 1250°C (shown on the dark-coloured clay). You can see here which have formed effective glazes at which temperatures, and which have not.

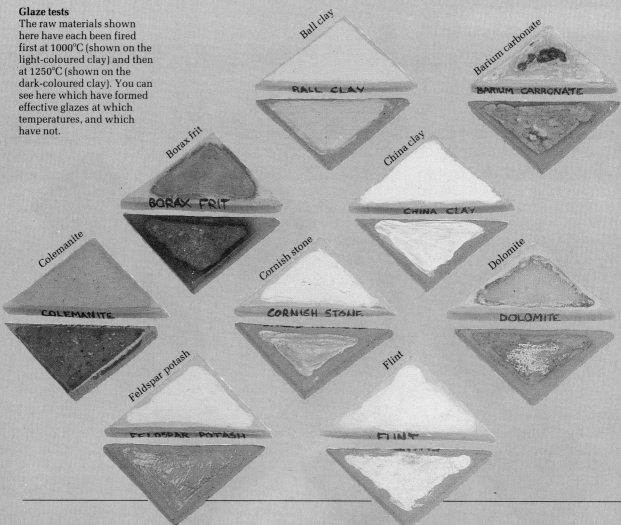

Feldspar and whiting
Dolomite and red clay
Feldspar and colemanite
Feldspar and magnesium carbonate
Feldspar and red clay

Test	1	2	3	4	5
Material A	100	75	50	25	0
Material B	0	25	50	75	100

Having established roughly the right proportions, experiment again more accurately. For example, if 50/50 seems about right, try 55/45, 45/50, 60/10, 40/60 and so on.

Next, experiment with mixtures of three materials. Try the following in different proportions:

Feldspar potash, whiting and flint
Feldspar potash, dolomite and china clay
Cornish stone, whiting and china clay
Nepheline syenite, whiting and ball clay

Try painting colouring oxides (see pp136-7) on to the clay surface under the glazes to see the effects that are created. Colourants can also be mixed with the glaze itself. You should also experiment with incorporating woodash into your glaze mixtures. Although woodash may itself form a glaze, it can also be combined with local or red clay to produce an attractive variety of different glazing effects.

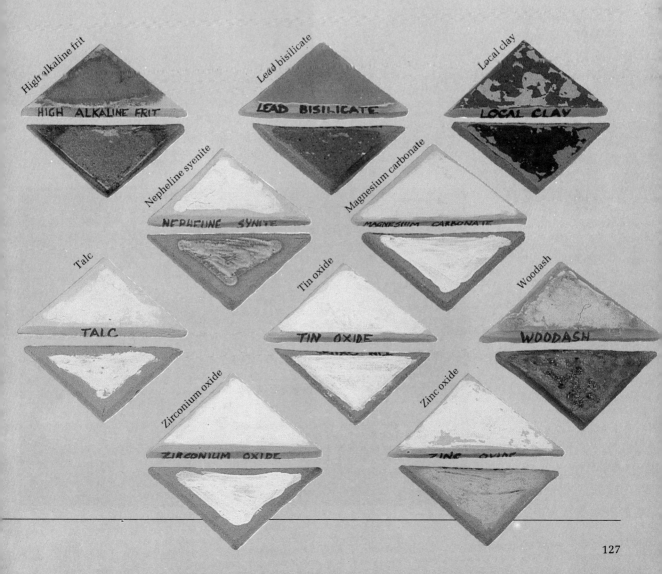

Decorative techniques/1

The colour and surface texture of fired clay can be altered very early in the clay preparation stages by adding various materials. Grog and sand (see pp42-3) can be added to give clay an attractively coarse texture. Combustible materials can also be used to create pitted or grained surfaces. To alter the colour of the clay, it can be mixed with colouring oxides (see pp136-7), stains or other types of clay.

Colouring oxides

Small amounts of colouring oxides will produce subtle colours which are worth some experimentation. A glaze is usually necessary to bring out the full colouring effect of the oxide.

Colouring oxides are expensive and, although the colours they produce when mixed with clay are distinctive, there are more economical ways of colouring your work if you are working on a large scale. For example, you may find that you can create the effect you require by using coloured slips (see pp136-9) or glazes (see pp122-7). However, small amounts of clays coloured with oxides are useful for inlay (see p134).

Before adding an oxide to the clay, mix it with a little water – this helps it combine more easily with the clay. Having kneaded the clay, slice it with a potter's harp, spread the resulting paste over the slices of clay, and then continue kneading. (For the quantities of oxide necessary and resultant colours, see pp146-7.)

Altering clay texture
A smooth surface texture is not always in keeping with the effect you wish to create.

Experiment with various additives to see the many different types of surface textures they will produce.

Pottery by Marian Gaunce and Dorothy Feibleman
A variety of patterns can be produced by combining different-coloured clays. The sources of Marian Gaunce's designs (centre) lie in rocks, patterned cloth and wood. Dorothy Feibleman's work (left and right) reflects her interest in furniture design.

Press-moulded slab pot by Peter Cosentino
Red powdered clay and crushed housebricks were added to the crank mixture used for this pot to create a warm colour and texture. ◁

Agateware
The patterns of agateware never reproduce themselves. Even when taken from one block of clay, the different-coloured layers can fall in an endless number of variations. ▽

The addition of oxides in any great quantity will tend to lower the temperature tolerance of the clay, so the pottery will not be able to withstand high firing temperatures. This means that you must take special care if you intend to fire at stoneware temperatures (see pp106-7). Bloating, where fired clay develops bulges in its structure during the firing (see Fault finding), may also occur if too high a percentage of oxide is added.

Agateware and neriage

One of the easiest and cheapest methods of altering a clay's colour is by blending it thoroughly with a lighter or darker one. Clay bodies of variegated colour can also be produced by wedging alternate layers of different – coloured clays together. The clay can then be used for throwing to produce a piece of work that gives a layered effect like agate – hence the name agateware. The quality of the surface will not be fully revealed until the pot is leatherhard and has been turned.

More complex colour effects can be produced by cutting layers of different-coloured clays into strips or small sections. Roll or fold these into whatever shape or size you wish, press them together into one block and wedge the clay. As the block is sliced off in thin sections, it will reveal complex colour patterns within the clay – an effect known as neriage. The clay may then be used for any hand-forming method or press-moulding (see pp70-3).

Adding combustible materials

Combustible materials, such as rice, wheat and sawdust, are mixed into the clay during kneading in the same way as grog or sand. They burn away during firing to leave small holes or indentations in the clay surface; the larger the particle size, the larger the indentations will be. You can combine several different combustible materials and mix them with the clay to give the surface more irregular markings. This technique is particularly effective for decorating large pieces of pottery.

Decorative techniques/2

Impressed decoration
You can decorate clay by impressing its surface while it is soft enough to take a clear impression without cracking but is no longer sticky. Pots can be impressed with random or regular patterns in various ways.

Using textured materials
Slabs of clay can be rolled over a textured material, such as hessian, rough netting, corrugated cardboard or even irregular strips of torn card. The pattern of the material will be transferred to the clay. The impressed slab can then be used to make various types of slab constructions (see pp66-7). Interesting tiles can also be made by decorating sheets of clay with a variety of impressed designs. The tiles are then cut to the required size from the textured clay (see p61).

Clay stamps and seals
Clay stamps, which can be used to impress patterns on a soft clay surface, can be made quite easily. To do this, roll out one or two clay coils of various widths and cut them into sections 3-4cm (1⅕-1⅗in) long. Take each coil section in turn and, using a sharp knife or pointed tool, cut the pattern or design of your choice on to one end of the coil. Bear in mind that the raised parts of the pattern on the actual stamp will become indentations in

the clay surface that you will decorate. Allow the stamps to dry thoroughly and then biscuit fire them.

Making a personalized stamp
You can make a stamp bearing your personal monogram or symbol. This can be used to mark and identify your work, which is particularly useful if you attend busy pottery classes. Try exploring designs based upon various combinations of your initials until you find a monogram you like. Carve or incise this into the end of one of your coil sections. Remember that to produce the correct image of a letter on a clay surface, the stamp must be incised with the letter's reverse image.

Embossed decoration
Stamps can be used to create embossed, as well as impressed, decoration, but there is little difference between the two techniques. For embossing, a soft pad of clay is attached to the surface of the pot when it is leatherhard, using a little slurry. The pad of clay can then be impressed with a stamp as usual and smoothed carefully with a sponge if necessary.

Decorative rollers
Repeating or regular patterns can be produced on clay slabs (see p60), using decorative rollers. To make the

Impressed decoration
This can be used to great effect on simple forms and shapes. It is particularly good for slab work where the clay surface is decorated before a piece of work is constructed.

rollers, make up some plaster (see p70-1) and pour it into cardboard tubes cut to a suitable size. The plaster sets inside the tube to form plaster pillars. When the plaster is completely dry, peel away the card tube and carve the design or pattern of your choice into the plaster surface. Blow away any plaster dust until the roller is completely clean.

Roll the roller across the clay slab, applying a gentle but firm pressure. The pattern on the roller will be repeated after each revolution.

You can also make decorative rollers from thick coil sections. Leave the coils until the clay is leatherhard before carving the design in them. Then make a small hole in each end with a pointed tool to a depth of at least 0.5cm (⅕in). Biscuit fire the coils and then fit a wire handle in the holes at each end to make the rollers easier to use.

Beating or paddling
Surface textures can be built up by hitting soft-leatherhard clay repeatedly with an object, such as an ordinary kitchen fork, an old hairbrush or a kitchen grater. Sticks and pieces of flattened wood or paddles can also be used. Try experimenting with a variety of different objects. Take care that you do not damage the structure of your pot.

Rolled decoration
Even the simplest of line patterns carved into a roller can create an exciting surface design.

Impressed decoration

Beating
You can create a variety of beaten patterns using one piece of wood as a beating tool. The pattern can be regular or irregular and can run horizontally or vertically over the clay surface.

Stamping
Support the pot with one hand and press the stamp into the clay.

Embossing
Having applied the soft pad of clay, press the stamp into it.

Decorative techniques/3

Cut surface decoration

This technique can be used to produce designs or patterns with sharp, clear lines, by cutting into the surface of a pot with a sharp tool. Try experimenting with a variety of blades and points, such as knives, pins, combs or hacksaw blades.

Incised decoration

Cutting into the clay surface with a single blade or point is usually referred to as incising. The sharpness of the lines will be determined not only by the tool you use but also the dryness of your clay. A wooden point will produce a far softer line than a metal one; incising a design on a newly-thrown pot will create a softer image than the same design on a leatherhard surface.

Incised decoration may consist of single lines cut into the clay or whole areas cut away from the surface to produce designs in relief – or a combination of both. Incised decoration is particularly useful if you wish to trace and transfer a design *(see pp34-5)*. When you have marked the outlines of the design on to the appropriate clay surface, they can then be incised with a sharp point or knife. You can then leave the design as it is or colour it with colouring oxides or slip *(see pp136-7)*.

Incised decoration
Incised lines can be used to add definition to different areas of colour in a design.

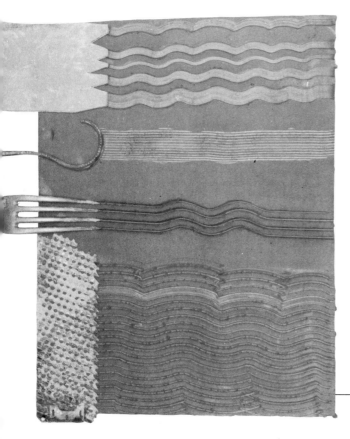

Combing

The surface of a pot can be combed with a fork, plastic hair comb, hacksaw blade or even with a piece of stiff card with teeth cut along one edge to produce sharp parallel lines. You will find that burrs are formed along the edges of the lines as you draw the combing tool through the clay. These can be removed with a stiff dry brush as soon as the clay is dry enough to allow you to do this without the crispness of the lines being affected.

Fluting

This involves cutting flat, slanted, concave or convex decorative grooves into the clay surface in horizontal, vertical or spiralling lines. For fluting very soft clay surfaces, you can use the end of a ruler or a wooden modelling tool. For slightly stiffer clay, or to create a more clearly-defined effect, you should use a sharp metal tool.

Straight-sided, hand-formed pots are easier to flute than rounded ones, but thrown pots can be fluted on the wheel during the throwing process. To make a fluted thrown shape, you should first throw a thick cylinder.

Combing
It is worth experimenting with almost any type of pointed edge to see the incised effect it will produce. You can cut your own combs with teeth of various shapes from pieces of stiff cardboard.

Then, with a ruler, carefully measure and lightly mark around the circumference of the cylinder the points at which you intend to make your grooves – these can be positioned at regular or irregular intervals. On the whole, fluting is most effective if it is contained within a band rather than covering the entire pot. Cut the grooves cleanly and confidently, using a ruler as a guide if necessary.

When you have finished fluting you can continue to shape the cylinder as you wish, although you must be careful not to touch the outside fluted surface as you work. The cylinder can be swelled to make an attractive bowl or, if you leave a thickened rim on the cylinder when you throw it, this can be raised and collared to make a fluted bottle.

Faceting
Facets can be cut around the sides of thrown pots. However, it is advisable that any pot you intend to facet has thick walls so that there is no danger of weakening the structure or piercing the clay. Faceting can be done just after throwing has been completed, while the clay is still soft, with a cutting wire or a small potter's harp. Otherwise the facets can be cut with a sharp knife once the clay is leatherhard.

Faceting
Facets should be cut in one clean, confident movement with a taut cutting wire.

Applied surface decoration
This involves applying more clay to the surface of a completed pot to build up a design in relief. Patterns can be formed from small coils or pellets of clay, which you attach to the pot's surface with thick slurry. Alternatively, larger pieces of clay can be fixed to the surface and then modelled to create a design in sculptural relief. You can decorate the entire surface of a pot in this way, or concentrate on smaller areas.

Fluting a rounded thrown bowl

1 Throw a thick cylinder about 15cm (6in) wide and 15cm (6in) high. Using a sharp point, mark a central band around the pot 1cm (2/5in) in from the base and rim. Mark the required widths of the facets around the rim and base. Cut each groove from the bottom upwards, using a ruler as a guide. ◁

2 When the △ fluting is complete, rotate the wheel and swell the cylinder from the inside to form a bowl. Do not touch the outside surface.

3 Provided that ◁ you leave a thick rim on your thrown form, you can continue to shape and develop your work after fluting is complete.

Decorative techniques/4

Sprig decoration

Repetitive clay patterns or motifs, made in miniature moulds *(see pp70-3)*, can be applied to the surface of a piece of work when it is leatherhard. Sprig decoration can be made either from the same clay as the body of the work or from a different-coloured clay. Wedgewood jasperware is the most well-known example of this type of sprig decoration, with its white motifs mounted on a background of the coloured clay body.

To make the sprig mould, carve the negative image of your required design or motif into a piece of plaster. Blow away the dust from the mould and make sure it is clean. Press a small piece of clay into the mould and cut the surface flush with that of the mould. Remove the clay from the mould by attaching a small piece of plastic clay to it to serve as a handle and then drawing it out. Score the area to which the sprig is to be attached and fix it in place with a little slurry.

Keep your designs simple and compact – this ensures that they will not disintegrate as you extract them from the plaster mould.

Pierced decoration

A pattern or design can be pierced through the walls of a pot once the clay is leatherhard – the clay should be

Sprig decoration
1 Press the motifs from a plaster mould. △

2 Fix them in place with a little slurry. ▷

Pierced bowl by Peter Lane
This thrown porcelain bowl was pierced when the clay was leatherhard to reduce the risk of distorting the shape. The pierced design represents a ring of trees. ▷

dry enough to withstand pressure applied by the piercing tool without warping, while being sufficiently plastic not to split. For piercing, use a very sharp scalpel blade or a proprietary piercing tool.

Small holes can be made in thin clay walls by pressing items, such as grains of wheat or rice, into the clay while it is still soft. These grains burn away during firing to leave either tiny holes or deep impressions, which also add to the overall decorative effect. Bear in mind that although a pattern that involves extensive piercing may be very attractive, too many holes will weaken the structure of a pot.

Inlay

When a pot is leatherhard, thin channels or lines can be cut into the clay surface. This can be done using a lino cutting tool, which can be bought at most art supply shops. The channels can then be filled with a different-coloured clay to the body of the pot. To make the inlay, take a suitable quantity of the same type of clay that has been used for the body of the pot and alter its colour by adding the appropriate amount of colouring oxides. This will ensure that the inlay will shrink at the same rate as the rest of the pot during drying and firing, and that no cracks or splits will appear.

To apply the inlay, brush a little water into the groove and press the inlay firmly into place. Leave the inlay until it becomes leatherhard and then scrape the surface clean with a metal kidney or blade to reveal the inlay as a well-defined line.

Burnishing

Once clay becomes leatherhard it can be polished to produce a smooth, shiny surface. This is done by rubbing the clay with a smooth object, such as the back of a spoon, a wooden modelling tool, knife blade or even your fingers. Rub the clay using small circular movements, working steadily over the entire surface.

Fine clays are best for burnishing, although fine-coloured slips can be applied over coarser clays. Burnishing is most effective on pots with simple and uncomplicated shapes (see p10).

A burnished pot can be sawdust-fired (see pp52-3) to produce an effective mottled grey/black surface colour, either instead of a normal biscuit firing or after one simply to 'smoke' the pot. Burnished pots are best biscuit fired at a low temperature because the shine tends to diminish as the temperature increases. After firing the surface should be polished again. A burnished pot will not be watertight.

Inlay
1 Mark out the design with a pointed tool.

2 Channel out the lines for the inlay using a lino cutting tool.

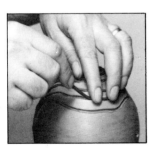

3 Gently press the inlay into the incised lines.

4 Scrape the surface when the clay is leatherhard.

Inlay design
Here, the lines of inlay complement the rounded shape of the pot.

Decorative techniques/5

Colouring the clay surface
Ceramic colourants, such as underglaze colours, body and glaze stains and specially-prepared metal oxides, are generally referred to as colouring oxides. They are available from pottery suppliers in powdered form and can be used to colour the clay at various stages during the pottery process. They can be added to the clay while it is being prepared *(see pp42-3)* to alter the natural colour of the clay body. This is expensive, however, if large amounts of clay are involved; so the most popular and economical way to colour clay is to coat its surface with a colouring oxide. Slip – clay in liquid form – can also be mixed with a colouring oxide and then applied to the clay surface.

Preparing a coloured slip
If the clay you normally work with is light-coloured, you can use it as the base for all but white or very light-coloured slips. The slip can be coloured by adding the required percentage of colouring oxide *(see pp146-7)*.

Weigh out the amount of dry powdered clay you need into a suitable plastic bowl or bucket. Add the appropriate amount of colourant. Gradually pour water over the dry ingredients, stirring the mixture well until it is the consistency of a thin paste.

If you do not have any ready-prepared powdered clay, you can prepare your own by rolling out thin sheets of clay, leaving them to dry and then crushing them to a powder.

Experimenting with slip
The same colour slip can look quite different, depending on the glaze used over it, so you should try using various combinations of slips and glazes. White, green, blue, brown and black slip are shown here, first by themselves *(1)*, and then under transparent glaze *(2)*; gloss white glaze *(3)*; and matt white glaze *(4)*.

Place two pieces of wood across another bowl or container and place a 60 or 90 sieve on top of them. Pass the mixture through the sieve with a lawn brush. Stir the slip well before you apply it.

Painting oxides on to dry, fired or glazed surfaces
Oxides can be mixed with water and then painted on to dry clay, biscuit ware or freshly-glazed pots. Since the powdered colourants are heavy in relation to the water and are likely to separate, stir the mixture before each brushstroke. If the pot is to be fired at earthenware temperatures, the oxide must be covered by a suitable glaze to fix it properly. However, oxides can be used by themselves on pots fired at stoneware temperatures.

Colouring glazes
Colouring oxides can also be used to colour glazes, and can be added to the glaze mixture at the preparation stages *(see pp116-7 and 124-5)*. They can also be brushed or sprayed over glaze before it is fired.

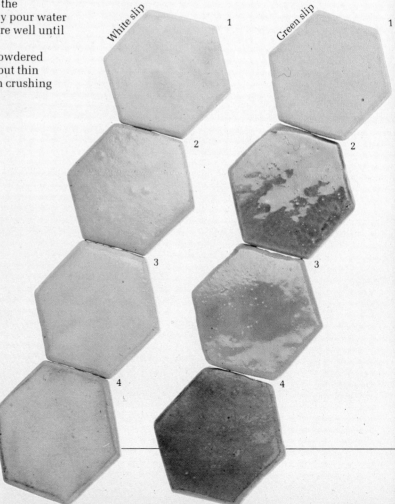

White slip 1

Green slip 1

2

2

3

3

Normal fired clay

4

4

The four main colourants

These are available in the form of oxides, carbonates or both. Oxides are usually stronger than carbonates. They are also coarser grained, and so are likely to produce a speckle in glazes or slips. Subtle colours can be produced by combining small amounts of other oxides with the main colourant.

Iron oxide

Iron oxide is available in a variety of forms. Red iron oxide is the most popular, although iron chromate, black iron oxide, purple iron oxide (also referred to as crocus matis), spangles and yellow ochre are also available. It is the most important colouring oxide, since it is capable of providing a wide variety of colour under different firing temperatures or when used in conjunction with particular glazes or other oxides.

At earthenware temperatures quantities of up to four per cent will produce beautiful amber and honey glazes when lead is present.

At stoneware temperatures iron oxide can be applied directly to stain the clay surface producing red brown to dark brown hues – this is particularly effective for highlighting textured surfaces or sculptural pieces without obscuring any detail. The addition of between two to ten per cent of iron oxide in stoneware glaze produces light tans, rich red browns and even blacks. Iron oxide can also be mixed with other oxides to produce other colour variations.

Cobalt carbonate and cobalt oxide

Cobalt is the most powerful colourant and produces various shades of blue under different conditions. You should be careful not to get any cobalt on your hands while you are preparing or using it, as you may inadvertently leave blue fingerprints on the clay surface, which will show clearly after firing.

Cobalt tends to produce harsh blues when used by itself, but when mixed with a little iron, manganese or copper, more subtle colours will result. If cobalt is used

Decorative techniques/6

in a glaze containing magnesium, it will produce a purple hue.

If cobalt is applied by itself to the clay surface and fired at stoneware temperatures, it will create a dark slate-coloured metallic finish. Cobalt can be mixed with manganese and iron to produce rich black slips.

Copper carbonate and copper oxide

On its own, copper is an ineffective surface colourant, producing a dull tea-stain colour, so it should always be covered with glaze. On clay fired in an electric kiln, copper produces a range of greens from pale to dark apple green. When it is used in large amounts, it creates gun metal black. In glazes with a strong alkaline content it produces turquoise blues. When fired in a solid fuel kiln, shades of red may result.

Copper carbonate and copper oxide are potentially dangerous substances. They should not be used in low lead soluble glazes (see pp122-3) if the pots are to be used as containers for food and drink.

Manganese dioxide and manganese carbonate

As a glaze colourant, manganese produces a range of colours varying from pinky mauve to purple or brown, depending on the other ingredients used in the glaze. By itself, manganese produces an attractive brown with tiny metallic specks at stoneware temperatures. Manganese dioxide, which is coarser grained than manganese carbonate, produces a more pronounced speckled effect.

Manganese is a useful colourant to mix with other oxides. When combined with iron, it produces rich browns; when mixed with cobalt, it creates a variety of violets, purples and plums.

Other metal colouring oxides

Antimony, chromium and nickel oxides are also used as colourants, but cannot be relied upon to behave predictably throughout the temperature range. All three oxides are poisonous and should be treated with great care (see pp48-9).

Colourants and glazes
The four main colouring oxides are shown here, first on an unglazed surface (1), and then under transparent glaze (2); gloss white glaze (3); and matt white glaze (4).

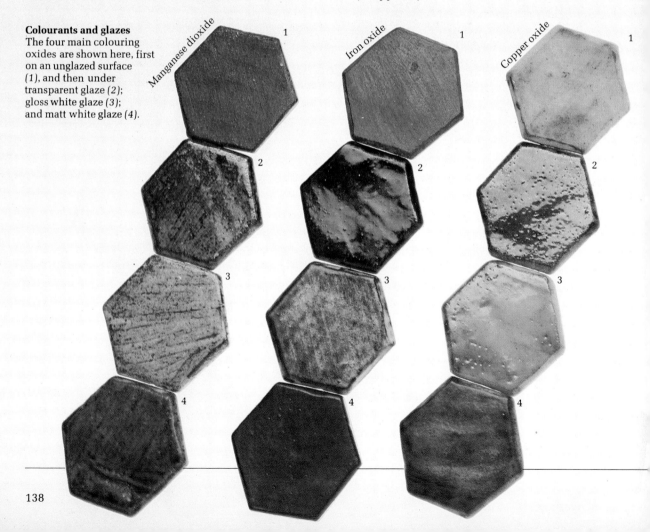

Antimony oxide
This is used in high-lead glazes to produce Naples yellow in earthenware glazes. It is effective in amounts of up to 15 per cent in glazes.

Chromium oxide
At stoneware temperatures, chromium oxide produces a dull lifeless colouring in both slips and glazes. However, when it is used at low earthenware temperatures in lead glazes, it will produce yellows and reds. If it is combined in quantities of up to three per cent with tin oxide, it produces an attractive pink-coloured chrome glaze.

Nickel oxide
This produces muted browns and greys when used by itself. However, it is usually used to modify other colours – for example, it will soften a normally harsh cobalt blue to a more delicate blue-grey. Nickel oxide should be used in quantities up to three per cent.

How much colourant to use
You only need to use a very small quantity of a colouring oxide to alter the colour of a glaze, slip or clay quite considerably. There are no hard and fast rules about how much colourant you should use. However, the chart of colouring oxides (see pp146-7) provides a guide to the approximate percentage of each colourant to use in glazes, slips and clay bodies, and the range and type of colour each will be expected to produce in given circumstances.

The effects of each colourant depend on various factors – the type of kiln you use, the firing temperature, whether the colourant is used by itself or in conjunction with other colourants. The colour an oxide produces will also depend on whether it is used in a glaze or a slip, or painted under or over a glaze. It is important that you experiment with all of these variations, trying them out in different contexts. Keep a careful record of the results of all your tests, as you will find that these are useful for future reference.

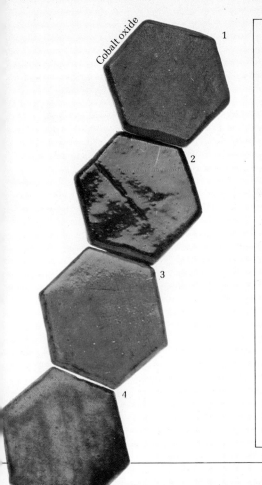

Cobalt oxide

1

2

3

4

Slip recipes

The following recipes are particularly useful if you usually work with a clay that is too dark in colour to form a good base for coloured slips. The quantities of each ingredient are given here in their proportional percentages of the total weight.

On the whole, slip is best applied when the clay is leatherhard. However, the recipes given here can be used on dry clay provided that the slip is applied quite thinly.

White slip
Ball clay 65
China clay 35

Green slip
Add 1-5% copper oxide to the above recipe for pale to medium green.

Blue slip
Add ½-1½% cobalt oxide to the above recipe for a pale to deep blue.

Brown slip
Red earthenware clay 100

Black slip
Red earthenware clay 85
Manganese dioxide 10
Red iron oxide 5

For example, to make medium green slip you would mix together ball clay, china clay and copper carbonate. To make brown slip use red clay, and for black slip use red clay, manganese and iron oxide.

Decorative techniques/7

Dipping and pouring
These are the easiest methods of applying a coloured slip to a pot. The pot is allowed to dry until it is leatherhard; it can then be dipped into a bucket of slip or, if this is not possible, slip can be poured over or in it. The techniques of dipping and pouring slip are the same as those of dipping and pouring glaze (see pp118-9). Both of these techniques offer a variety of decorative possibilities.

Slip trailing
Traditional slip trailing techniques have recently regained popularity and offer a marvellous range of decorative possibilities. You can use proprietary slip trailers but empty, cleaned washing-up liquid bottles are a cheap alternative. If you use washing-up bottles make the slip quite thick, as the nozzles are slightly larger than those of slip trailers.

Shallow press-moulded plates or dishes are ideal for slip trailing. You may also try decorating a flat sheet of clay, and then cutting the sections you need from this as soon as the slip decoration is dry enough to be handled without being damaged.

Fill the trailer with slip and hold the nozzle just above the clay surface. Allow the slip to flow out in a continuous stream as you move the trailer over the clay. Until you gain in confidence, your movements may be hesitant and your lines unsure, so it is worth practising first on paper to get used to the speed at which the slip flows from the trailer.

You can trail slips directly on to leatherhard clay surfaces, or you can first cover the surface with slip and then trail a slip pattern into this while it is still wet. This means that the trailed slip runs slightly into the background colour. You can also try experimenting with patterns built up from dots.

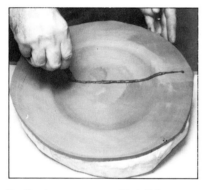

Feathering a press-moulded dish
1 Before you trim the dish, trail slip lines across the surface.

2 The lines should all be parallel and should run right across the dish from edge to edge.

3 If you wish, you can trail lines of a different-coloured slip in between the first lines.

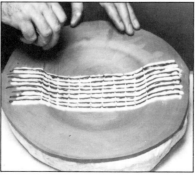

4 Draw a pin across the lines at right angles. Trim excess clay from the edge of the dish when the slip is dry.

Combing
Apply a coat of slip to the pot and draw your fingers across it to create thick wavy lines.

Marbling
1 Apply blobs of different-coloured slips at random.

2 Give the pot several quick, sharp jerks so that the slips run to give a marbled effect.

Feathering
Carefully trail parallel lines of slip across the clay surface. Draw a pin, needle or pointed tool across the slip at right angles to the lines to create a feathered effect. Traditionally the tip of a feather was used for this technique from which it has derived its name.

Try feathering surfaces using one, two or more colours. You should take great care not scratch into the clay surface as you draw the needle through the slip, as this will spoil the pattern by giving it an uneven and ragged appearance.

Combing
Cover the clay surface completely with a coloured slip. Draw your fingers through it while it is still wet to create a pattern on the surface by revealing the clay underneath. You can also try the same technique using two different-coloured slips. Apply the first and allow it to stiffen slightly. Then apply the second slip and draw your fingers through it as before. Card combs, cut with different-sized and shaped teeth, can also be used for this technique.

Marbling
Pour blobs of different-coloured slips at random on to a leatherhard clay surface and then move the pot around in several jerky movements before the slips have a chance to dry. The slips will swirl and mix together to create a marbled pattern.

Once-fired slipware by Alan Frewin
This attractive collection of domestic ware shows how slip trailers can be used effectively to 'paint' the most sophisticated patterns and even pictures.

Decorative techniques/8

Brushed slip decoration

If it is impractical to coat a piece of work with slip by the usual methods of dipping and pouring, the slip can be applied with a brush. Slip can be brushed over impressed decoration to heighten the textural contrasts between the pattern and the rest of the clay surface, or it can be used by itself to paint a design. A wide variety of brushes are available from pottery suppliers – the Japanese ranges are particularly good.

Before you begin to paint, make sure that the brush is well loaded with slip so that it does not run dry in mid-stroke. Remember that simple, bold lines are usually the most effective.

Colouring oxides and glazes can also be used for all forms of brushed decoration, having been prepared in the usual way *(see pp136-7, pp116-7 and pp124-5).* However, oxides should be applied to the pot when the clay is dry or biscuit fired; glazes are normally applied after biscuit firing.

Banding

Lines or bands of slip are best painted on to a thrown pot just after it has been trimmed. If you wish to produce slightly softer lines, the bands can be applied to a newly-thrown pot while the clay is plastic. In both cases, work while the pot is still on the wheel.

If the pot is not already on the wheel, you can recentre it again or put it on a bench whirler. Dip the brush into the slip, making sure that it holds sufficient slip to paint the band around the circumference of the pot. Support your right hand with your left and tuck your elbows in or rest them on a suitable surface so that you can produce a steady line. Start the wheel, holding the brush against the clay until a complete band has been drawn.

Banding by itself is a somewhat clinical form of decoration, but it can provide an effective framework for freehand brushwork or other types of decoration. Try experimenting with various combinations. You should also try banding with different colours.

Resist decoration

Patterns can be created in relief on the clay surface, using a resist to prevent the slip touching the clay when the pot is coated. A variety of materials and objects are suitable for use as resists. If the clay is still soft enough to be impressed, you can press a selection of different *objets trouvés*, such as keys, coins, paper clips, cords, string and fabrics, into the surface of the clay and then brush a good coating of coloured slip over them. The combination of impressed and resist decoration will effectively heighten the design.

Pot by Henry Hammond
This simple and lively brushwork design displays the potter's masterly use of the technique. ▷

Banding
This can be carried out on the wheel or on a bench whirler.
▽

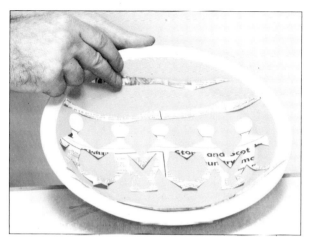

Paper resists
A repeating pattern resist can
be made in the same way as a
child's paper chain.

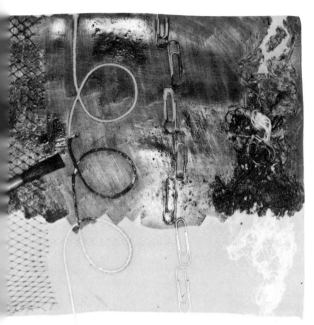

Resists
Try to gather a varied
collection of *objets trouvés* to
use as resists.

Paper resist

Paper patterns or stencils cut from newspaper can also be used as resists. These can be cut to produce regular repeating patterns or pictorial designs. To transfer the resist, cut out your required design, dampen the paper with a little water and press it firmly on to the surface of the clay.

Wax resist

Wax is the most popular material for resists and although you can make it yourself by mixing melted candle wax with a little paraffin, it is easier to buy a proprietary emulsion from pottery suppliers. The emulsion will last almost indefinitely, provided the container is always sealed properly. Slips and oxides can be applied over a wax resist, but the technique is most commonly used with glaze after biscuit firing, or with a second application of glaze or oxide over the first coat of glaze. The wax burns away during firing to leave a characteristic finish in the resist areas of tiny blobs of slip, glaze or oxide.

You should not use glaze over a wax resist directly on the surface if the pot is to be fired at earthenware temperatures and is intended to hold food or drink. This is because the resist areas will still be porous, even after the final firing.

Applying a wax resist

Paint on the emulsion and leave it to dry. Apply the slip, oxide or glaze over the resist. If you are using slip, make sure it is not too thick or it will penetrate the wax.

Decorative techniques/9

Sgraffito

This is the technique of scratching a design through a coating of slip, glaze or oxide to reveal the surface beneath it. It may involve scratching through a single coating of colour to expose the clay itself, or applying two coats of different-coloured slips, glazes or oxides to a pot and then scratching through the top coating to reveal the colour beneath it. You can use any sharp point for sgraffito, but needles, pointed steel modelling tools and knives are the most commonly-used tools.

You can use traced designs or templates as a basis for sgraffito work (see pp34-5), or work freehand if you wish. You can also combine sgraffito with combing techniques (see pp132-3).

Smoking

This is a simple decorative technique which produces beautiful variations in shades of grey to black. It is particularly effective when used in combination with a very smooth clay, such as a red-bodied type or porcelain, which has been burnished (see pp134-5) to a high shine prior to firing.

Pottery can be smoked by firing it in a simple sawdust kiln (see pp52-3). This is easy and quick to build. However, as sawdust kilns are only capable of reaching very low firing temperatures, they are rarely suitable for biscuit firing. It is therefore best to biscuit fire your pottery first in an electric kiln as you would normally (see pp108-11), and then to fire it again in a sawdust kiln to create the distinctive smoked effect.

Post-biscuit decoration

There are various ways of decorating pottery after it has been biscuit fired. On the whole, painted decoration is the most practical, as by now the clay is no longer soft or impressionable.

Sgraffito

A coating of coloured oxide can be scratched through to reveal the clay.

You can use two glazes and scratch through the second to reveal the first.

Smoked pot by Karen Hessenberg
This thrown porcelain bowl was smoked to produce the subtle grey-black colouring.

Underglaze decoration

Colours – either in the form of slips, oxides or specially-created colours – that are applied to the clay surface after it has been biscuit fired and are then coated with glaze are known as underglaze colours. Applying colour to the clay at this stage has advantages over applying colour before firing. Unfired clay is extremely fragile, while colours can be easily smudged when the pot is handled. Also, great care must be taken when such pots are loaded in the kiln for biscuit firing; they must also be placed further apart than usual, so that the surfaces do not touch.

Painting on the biscuit fired surface also has some disadvantages, because the clay is very porous and so absorbs slip or oxide very quickly. It is easy to apply too thick a coating, which may flake when it dries. Mistakes cannot be eradicated completely, because once the colour is absorbed, the surface is stained permanently. The coloured surface can also be easily smudged, and so glaze must be applied very carefully. Use a spray if possible (see pp120-1). Many potters also feel that an unfired clay surface reacts far better to brushwork, as the lines of colour merge slightly with the clay.

A large range of prepared underglaze colours are available from pottery suppliers. The colours are usually vivid – rarely subtle – but most of them can be mixed. They are available in crayon, powder and liquid forms, but it is most economical to buy the powdered form and then mix it with the specified mixing media. Although all the colours are guaranteed to be effective at normal earthenware temperatures, colours in the spectrum of yellow to red will often burn away before the stoneware temperature is reached. The manufacturer's catalogue will tell you the temperatures each colour will tolerate, so use this as your guide.

Many potters feel that an unfired clay surface reacts far better to brushwork, as the lines of colour merge slightly with the clay. Because the decoration is fixed by biscuit firing, pots can also be glazed easily. Mistakes can also be rectified when you are painting on to unfired clay, as they can simply be carefully scraped away with a sharp knife.

Metal colouring oxides as underglaze colours

Metal colouring oxides can be used as underglaze colours, although they are coarser than the proprietary underglaze colours. Oxides produce speckled colours, due to their coarseness. If you want to avoid this effect, mix the oxide powder with a little water and grind it as finely as possible in a mortar and pestle.

Oxides must, in any case, be mixed with a small amount of water before they are applied to a clay surface. The addition of a little gum arabic will help to bind the oxide to the pot.

Overglaze and majolica decoration

Colouring oxides can be used to paint a design on a glazed pot before the glaze firing, provided that the glaze you use is fairly light in colour. This type of decoration can be used on any clay at any temperature.

To apply overglaze decoration, give your pot an even coating of glaze. As soon as the glaze is absorbed, you can begin to paint. Before applying each brush stroke, remember to stir the colour mixture, as oxides and water tend to separate very quickly. Use bold confident strokes when applying the oxide, and bear in mind that the actual lines of each brushstroke will still be visible once the pot is fired. Resists, particularly those made of wax (see pp142-3), and banding can also be used for overglaze decoration.

Overglazed ware should be packed very carefully in the kiln for the glaze firing, as the decorated glaze surface is very fragile. If possible, when loading the kiln, hold the pots only from inside the neck and beneath the base.

Majolica decoration is one specific type of overglaze decoration. It involves the application of specially-prepared colouring oxides on to a biscuit fired clay surface, which has been freshly coated with white tin earthenware glaze.

Planter by Peter Cosentino
Copper, cobalt, manganese and ilmenite oxides were painted over a matt white glaze before firing. The different bands of colour clearly define the areas of applied clay decoration.

Common clay types and colourants

Type of clay	SiO_2	TiO_2	Al_2O_3	Fe_2O_2	CaO	MgO
Stoneware throwing	62.4	1.3	24.5	1.2	0.2	0.3
Craft crank	61.3	0.9	26.3	2.8	0.4	0.3
Light red	57.9	0.4	17.4	8.7	0.7	0.2
White earthenware	69.6	0.5	19.0	0.7	0.1	0.6
Porcelain	65.0	0.3	22.9	0.35	0.4	0.2
Raku	55.0	1.0	28.6	2.5	0.6	0.9

Colourant	Cobalt carbonate	Cobalt oxide	Copper carbonate	Copper oxide	Iron chromate	Black iron oxide
Recommended amount (Expressed as percentage of total volume of mixture)	½-3%	¼-2%	2-7%	1-5%	2-5%	4-8%
Resultant colour and effect	Pale to dark blue. Even texture. Not as strong as the oxide.	Pale to dark blue. Speckles some glazes. Creates purple in some glazes and a blue/grey metallic finish at 1250°C.	Pale to dark apple green. Produces an even-textured colour.	Pale to dark apple green. Slightly stronger than carbonate. Produces speckled effect.	Subdued grey/browns. Tones down other colours.	Cooler but stronger colours than other forms of iron.
General comments			Both forms of copper produce turquoise in some glazes and strong reds fired in combustible fuel-operated kilns. Large quantities make gun-metal black. By themselves, both forms only produce weak colours. Do not use in soluble lead glazes for food and drink containers.		These give a wide range of colours from pale tans to black. Red iron oxide is the most popular form. Iron is an active flux when added to a glaze. It produces a pleasant red/brown by itself on the clay surface when fired over 1250°C.	

K_2O	Na_2O	Content of other clays	Grog content	Texture	Fired colour	Vitrification point in °C	Firing range in °C
1.8	0.6	89%	11%	Smooth/Medium	Off white	1280-1300	1160-1290
1.4	0.6	26%	45%	Coarse	Brown buff (toast)	1280-1320	1170-1300
1.0	1.0	87%	0%	Smooth	Light red brown	1150-1170	1060-1150
2.0	1.5	70%	30%	Smooth	White	1200-1260	1100-1220
3.2	0.9	30%	0%	Smooth	White	1260-1310	1250-1340
2.3	0.2	0%	50%	Coarse	Brownish buff	1280-1330	900+

Purple iron oxide	Red iron oxide	Iron spangles	Yellow ochre	Manganese carbonate	Manganese dioxide
4-8%	2-15%	1-5%	3-8%	2-8%	2-10%
Range of tans and browns with speckled effects.	Range of colours from honey to dark brown. Produces mottled brown or yellow in ash glazes.	Metallic flecks in clays and glazes.	Range of colours from yellow to brown.	Range of colours from pinky mauve to brown. Creates an even colour in slips and glazes.	Range of colours from pinky mauve to brown. Fired above 1250°C, it creates dark brown. Produces a speckled effect.

Measuring techniques

When you are joining two or more parts of a pot together, it is important to measure each component accurately. Use a pair of calipers to do this, setting them to the required width, length or depth of the first component of the pot. For example, when fitting a lid, the calipers should be set to span the width of the inside rim of the pot. The lid is then made to these dimensions, the calipers being kept conveniently nearby for checking.

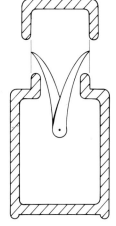

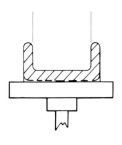

A cup lid
The diameter of the pot's outside rim should be equal to the diameter of the lid's inside rim.

Key

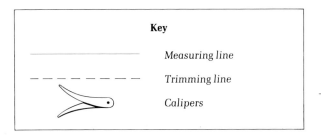

—————————— *Measuring line*

– – – – – – – – – *Trimming line*

Calipers

Joining thrown shapes

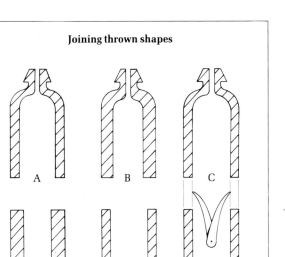

A   B   C

✗   ✗   ✓

When joining thrown forms together, it is not sufficient just to measure the diameters of the outside rims. It is vital that the walls of each

thrown section to be joined are of the same thickness. Otherwise, there is the risk that the join will crack open during drying or firing.

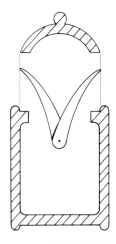

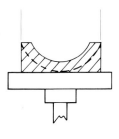

Simple bowl lid
The diameter of the pot's inside rim equals the diameter of the lid's outside rim after trimming.

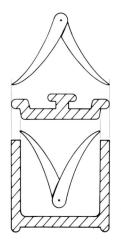

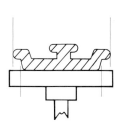

Flanged lid
The diameter of the lid's base equals the diameter of the pot's inside rim. The diameter of the lid's outside rim equals the diameter of the pot's outside rim.

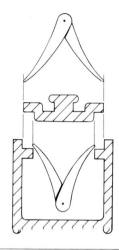

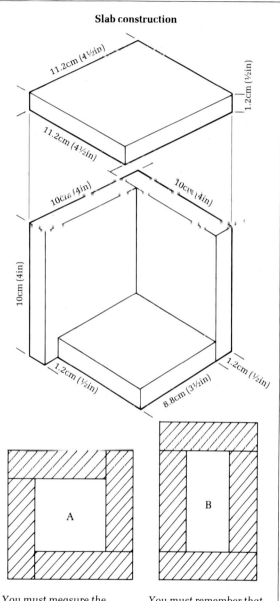

Slab construction

11.2cm (4½in)

1.2cm (½in)

11.2cm (4½in)

10cm (4in)

10cm (4in)

10cm (4in)

1.2cm (½in)

1.2cm (½in)

8.8cm (3½in)

Snug-fitting lid
The diameter of the lid's base equals the diameter of the pot's inside gallery. The diameter of the lid's outside rim equals the diameter of the pot's inside rim.

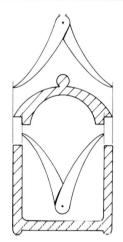

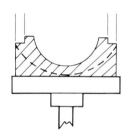

Flanged bowl lid
The diameter of the lid's outside rim equals the diameter of the pot's outside rim. The diameter of the lid's flange equals the diameter of the pot's inside rim.

A

B

Flanged lid with gallery
The diameter of the lid's outside rim equals the diameter of the pot's inside rim. The diameter of the lid's flange equals the diameter of the pot's inside gallery.

You must measure the width, length and depth of each slab component precisely to make sure they will fit together. For the best results, it is essential to calculate the measurements before you begin work.

You must remember that the way the slabs are joined together affects the proportions of the finished piece. For example, the square (A) and rectangle (B) above can be made from the four slabs of the same basic measurements.

Fault finding/1

Problem	Diagnosis	Solution
Clay sticks to fingers or work surface	Clay is too soft Surface is non-porous	Dry clay on plaster slab Cover work surface with newspaper
Unfinished work dries out excessively between working sessions	Water is evaporating too quickly from clay	Wrap unfinished work in polythene or place it in a damp cupboard. If you leave it for a long time, cover work with damp cloth and polythene
Cracks appear in work before biscuit firing	Work has dried out too quickly	Dry work more gradually. Keep work away from draughts or direct heat. Cover with polythene if necessary
Clay is not self-supporting	Clay is too wet and soft	Allow clay to dry
Clay cracks or splits during forming	Clay is too stiff and coarse	Use softer or finer clay

Pinching

Pinch spheres crack at join during drying	Two halves badly joined or no escape hole for enclosed air	If clay is not dry, score the rim again and join the two halves with slurry. Leave a tiny escape hole for air

Coiling

Coils become flat rather than round as they are rolled	Rolling action is uneven	Pat coils into round shape again and continue rolling, making sure you roll them through 360°
Coils develop a hollow section or crack as they are rolled	Clay too dry	Use softer clay
Coiled form collapses as it is widened or narrowed	Clay too soft to support its own weight	Use slightly stiffer clay Leave base section of work to stiffen before adding further coils Support narrowing forms from inside with crushed newspaper
Cracks appear along the line of coil joins	Coils are poorly joined	Merge coils into each other to form good joins
	Coils are of uneven thicknesses	Use coils of even thickness.
	Coils on half-finished work have been allowed to dry out too much for the fresh coils to be added	Use score marks and slurry to join the first of new coils to the base section
Coils stick to surface of former	Surface of former is non-porous Clay has shrunk during drying	Wrap newspaper around the former Remove former before the clay stiffens

Problem	Diagnosis	Solution
Slabbing		
Slab construction collapses	Clay too soft	Allow slab to stiffen slightly before you attempt construction
Slab sections crack during forming	Clay too dry	Use softer clay. If necessary, bend slab to required shape while wet and then allow it to stiffen before joining
Slab tears as it is lifted	Clay embedded in hessian Clay rolled out too thinly	Turn clay sheet frequently Roll thicker sheets
Slab warps during drying or firing	Slab is of uneven thickness Drying process too rapid Clay used was too plastic	Use wooden guides for rolling Dry slowly away from draughts or direct heat Add grog to clay to reduce plasticity
Sculpture		
Work collapses	Support too weak for weight of clay mass Centre of gravity misjudged	Make models more stable Choose postures with more support
Making moulds		
Plaster does not set	Plaster is old Mixture too watery	Use fresh plaster. Keep open plaster in airtight containers Add more plaster to mix
Plaster sticks to casting model	Plaster may be caught in undercuts Insufficient releasing agent used	Check mould for possible undercuts Use more releasing agent
Handles		
Handle tears or breaks	Uneven pressure exerted along handle length	Use less pressure and more even strokes
Handle cracks in the middle during drying	Handle dries more quickly than pot	Once attached, wrap polythene around the handle to slow down drying process
Handle joins crack open	Clay of handle wetter than that of pot	Use stiffer clay Make sure pot is still soft-leatherhard when you attach handle When handle attached dry out very slowly

Fault finding/2

Problem	Diagnosis	Solution
Handle develops unevenly	Hand position incorrect	Make sure you turn your wrist through 180° on each successive pull
Clay fractures during pulling	Clay inadequately prepared	Knead and wedge clay more thoroughly

Throwing

Problem	Diagnosis	Solution
Clay will not move to centre of wheelhead	Clay too far off-centre	Drag clay nearer to the centre of the wheelhead before you begin
	Clay too dry	Use softer clay
Clay will not stick to wheelhead	Wheelhead too wet	Dry wheelhead
Clay will not centre after coning	Clay too hard	Use softer clay
	Hand and arm position incorrect	Check position of arms and hands
	Hands released clay too suddenly	Relax pressure of hands gradually
	Clay slightly off-centre	Adopt final centring position
Form collapses when opened	Form opened beyond width of base	Spread clay further on wheelhead before opening it
		Do not open clay as far
	Water collects inside base	Sponge out water from inside base
Rim cracks as form is opened	Clay not properly prepared	Prepare clay more thoroughly
	Clay too stiff	Use softer clay
	Form opened too rapidly	Apply downward pressure on rim as you open out shape
		Trim with a pin or needle
Small peak is visible in the centre of the base	Thumb not positioned in centre properly when clay was opened	Make sure you push thumb vertically into centre of clay
	Thumb tip moved downwards rather than horizontally when inside base was formed	Ensure thumb tip moves in direct horizontal position when opening
		Remove peak with fingers, sponge or tool
Wall is thicker on one side than the other	Clay off-centre	Ensure clay is centred before you open it
Clay wall tears as it is raised	Too much clay being raised in one lift	Increase wall height gradually by small successive lifts
	Too much pressure applied during lift	Apply less pressure to the clay
Clay buckles during collaring	Clay wall too thin	Attempt collaring sooner
	Pressure too great or too sudden	Apply pressure gradually and increase speed of wheel a little
	Clay overworked	Use the minimum of water for lubrication to prevent clay tiring

Problem	Diagnosis	Solution
Uneven form develops from well-centred clay	Unsteady arm and body position	Rest arms on wheeltray for support or tuck elbows tightly into your sides
Clay wall collapses near base or middle as it is raised	Too much or uneven pressure applied to clay	Apply gradual and even pressure to the clay
	Wall thinned too much for weight of clay it has to support	Increase height with successive lifts
Form widens as its height is increased	Hands move outwards instead of directly upwards during lift	Check lift is strictly vertical
	Fingers not directly opposite each other during lift	Keep fingers directly opposite each other during lift
Wall fractures and collapses at base	Wall thinned too much for the amount of clay it has to support	Leave walls slightly thicker near base when throwing tallish pots
	Water has collected in base and weakened structure	Sponge out water from inside base regularly
Wire cuts through base when removing pot from wheelhead	Base too thin	Remember to leave a minimum thickness of 1cm ($^2/_5$in) for the base, 1.5cm ($^3/_5$in) for medium-sized pieces of work

Trimming

Problem	Diagnosis	Solution
Pot wobbles when placed on wheelhead	Uneven rim	Stand pot upright, re-centre, and trim rim with a pin. Alternatively, add soft coil of clay as temporary levelling padding
Pot cannot be re-centred correctly	Pot not properly centred when thrown	Try to re-centre the piece of work as accurately as possible. If necessary, re-centre only the area you are actually trimming
Rippled pattern – 'chattering' – develops on pot surface during turning	Turning tools blunt	Sharpen tools
	Tools held too loosely	Rest arms on wheeltray for support and grip tools more tightly
	Clay too dry	Trim before clay passes leatherhard state or dampen pot surface with sponge before turning
Base pierced during trimming	Base too thin	Check thickness of base before trimming
	Pressure of tool too hard	Add a false base made from a slab of clay of the same consistency and then re-trim

Fault finding/3

Problem	Diagnosis	Solution
Base is very uneven	Pot removed with slack cutting wire	Hold cutting wire more tautly in future
	Pot too dry or stiff to allow safe removal	Cut through base before clay stiffens too much
		Add clay to level base before turning
Trimming tool digs into pot surface	Pot not centred correctly	Check pot is correctly centred
	Tool held incorrectly	Use a more rounded or flat tool and check tool position
	Clay too soft	Leave pot to dry more thoroughly before trimming
Wall is thinner on one side than the other	Pot not centred correctly	If wall thickness allows, re-centre pot and re-trim

Biscuit firing

Work explodes or fractures badly	Work not dried properly before firing	Leave work to dry longer before firing and pre-heat load before firing
	Work too thick for rate of temperature rise	Hollow out thick sections of work
	Large pockets of air trapped in clay	Ensure there are escape passages for air pockets
	Work fired too quickly	Fire work very slowly up to 200°C and 600°C.
Work cracks open	Pockets of air trapped in clay	Leave escape passages for air from known air pockets
		When joining clay surfaces during working, make sure joins are firm – join by scoring and apply slurry when clay is no longer soft
A crater – 'spit-out' – appears in surface immediately or some time after firing, often revealing a white powdery lump underneath	Impurities in clay (often plaster)	Throw out worn plaster slabs and moulds
		Keep clay as free as possible from contamination by other materials
		Use more refined types of clay
Hairline fractures occur	Firing temperature too low (most likely to occur with stoneware clays)	Fire biscuit ware to 1000°C
	Drying too rapid	Make sure all ware is thoroughly dry before firing
	First firing stages too fast	Pre-heat and fire slowly

Problem	Diagnosis	Solution
Glazing		
Biscuit-fired work will not absorb glaze	Temperature of biscuit firing too high	Fire biscuit ware at a lower temperature Add gum to glaze mixture Warm pot before glazing and fire to higher temperature
Large bumps – 'bloating'– appear in the clay	Too much colourant, oxide or carbon trapped in clay Overfiring	Use less colourant Add grog to clay Include carbon soak in biscuit firing and/or fire to lower glaze temperature
Clay walls split when cullet has been used for decoration	Glass contracts and expands during firing at different rate to clay	Make clay walls thicker Use less cullet
Bare patches – 'crawling' – develop on the glaze surface, the glaze sometimes separating into beads or blobs	Oil, grease or dust on biscuit fired clay surface Glaze mixture contains too much plastic clay Glaze layer cracks prior to firing Glaze mixture too thick or applied too thickly	Wash dusty biscuit ware and allow it to dry before glazing. Always handle biscuit ware as little as possible Reduce plastic clay content of glaze and substitute part or all with china clay Add water to glaze Reduce thickness of glaze mixture
A fine network of cracks – 'crazing' – appears on glaze surface	Shrinkage rates of clay and glaze incompatible Underfired glaze or body Glaze applied too thickly	Increase silica content of glaze Fire to higher temperature Add water to glaze mixture
Splitting of glazed ware – 'dunting' – occurs	Heating up or cooling down too rapid Clay walls uneven	Heat and cool kiln more gradually around 200°C and 600°C. Do not open kiln door until temperature is below 200°C Add grog to body
Glazed surface is peppered with tiny holes – 'pinholing'	Glaze slightly underfired Firing too quick Air bubbles trapped in glaze Excess whiting in glaze	Fire glaze at a slightly higher temperature Soak the glaze Reduce the silica content of the glaze, add more flux or use less whiting
Glaze flakes from surface –'peeling', 'shelling' or 'shivering' – usually around edges, rims and handles	Clay contracts more than glaze	Lower the firing temperature slightly Reduce soaking period Add alkaline frit or other high expansion frit to glaze Reduce silica content in glaze

Index

Acknowledgements

The author and publisher would like to thank the
following people and organizations for their kind help
in the production of this book:

British Crafts Centre; Bubble Publicity Ltd;
Buckinghamshire County Museum; Crafts Council;
Craftsmen Potters Association; Mr A V Evershed
(Principal) and Mr R A Clarke (Head of Department),
Milton Keynes College; Fenny Lodge Gallery, Milton
Keynes; Potclays Ltd; Philip Sayer; The World of
Interiors.

The author and publishers would also like to thank the
following artists who contributed to the book:

Gordon Baldwin; Richard Batterham; Marjorie Bennett;
Maggie Angus Berkowitz; Audrey Blackman; Ruth and
Alan Barrett-Danes; Hilary Brock; Delan Cookson; Hans
Coper; Ruth Duckworth; Dave Edmonds; Dorothy
Feibleman; Marian Gaunce; Adrian Glew; Siddig
El'Nigoumi; Sheila Fournier; Valerie Fox; Ruth
Franklin; Alan Frewin; Suzie Gray; Jane Hamlyn; Henry
Hammond; Ewen Henderson; Karen Hessenberg; Peter
Lane; Graham Legge; Nicholas Marangos; Eric Mellon;
David Morris; Magdalene Odundo; Rebecca Peters; John
Pollex; Mary Rogers; Sabina Teuteberg; James Tower.